Know Your Real Self - A journey towards inner peace and freedom

Rachna Khemchandani

Copyright© Rachna Khemchandani

ISBN: 978-1537016979

First Edition: 2017, Second Edition: 2018

Price : $ 8.10

Publisher : CreateSpace Independent Publishing Platform -

An Amazon Company

"Silence is the language of god, all else is poor translation."
- **Rumi**

"Peaceful is the one who's not concerned with having more or less. Unbound by name and fame, he is free from sorrow from the world and mostly from himself." - **Rumi**

"Seek the wisdom that will untie your knot. Seek the path that demands your whole being." - **Rumi**

"Yesterday I was clever, so I wanted to change the world. Today I am wise, so I am changing myself." - **Rumi**

PREFACE

Initially I never had any intention of writing any blog or book but Amit Vashisht, who is one of the spiritual seekers and knows me since last ten years, told me that I must write a blog or book to share my experiences and knowledge with other seekers. That is when I decided to write the blog. After a few years of writing my blog, I got messages from many readers who told me that they got lot of clarity from the articles posted in my blog and they were greatly benefitted by it. Seeing this I felt that now the time has come to write this book and get it published so that this knowledge and experience can reach more and more people across the world. I have written this book with the intention to help all the true, honest and sincere seekers who are seeking answers on their spiritual path or seeking clarity, wisdom and guidance on their path to realize their true self – a journey towards experiencing higher states of consciousness, inner peace and inner freedom.

This book is not meant to promote or propagate any one particular spiritual path or guru. This book is not written to make any name or fame or money. It is only written and published to genuinely help people on the spiritual path. Whatever I have written in this book is based on what I have practiced, learnt, realized and experienced on my spiritual path in last 30 years with the guiding light and grace of all my four gurus (Shirdi Sai Baba, Paramhansa Yogananda, Osho and Avdhoot Baba Shivananda) and other spiritual teachers like Ekhart Tolle.

ACKNOWLEDGEMENT

I am grateful for all the blessings and grace that I have received from all my gurus, supreme consciousness/shiv and supreme energy/shakti because of which I was able to write this book. I only hope and pray to god, that this book helps all the spiritual seekers on their path, moving towards inner freedom, peace and supreme consciousness.

INTRODUCTION

About the author: My birth name is Rachna Khemchandani. My spiritual name is Shashwati. I have done my schooling from Loreto Convent in Lucknow, India. I did my graduation in arts from Lucknow University. I did my Masters in Business Administration from Jaipuria Institue of Management in Lucknow. I have worked as a training manager and soft skills trainer in the past. I left my job in 2005 when I decided to completely focus on my spiritual path. I was born in the year 1977 and from the very beginning I had spiritual inclination, devotion and bhakti. I became more serious towards my spiritual path when I was 18 years old and after that there was no looking back. I kept on moving ahead with more and more intensity and focus till I realized my true self and inner freedom. I am currently living in Bangalore, India and playing a role of a spiritual guide and teacher helping, guiding and teaching a few selected students who are on this spiritual path.

Purpose of the book: The main purpose to write this book is to provide clarity and guidance to all the spiritual seekers throughout the world. I got a strong intuitive feeling to write this book so that more and more people can be benefited by it. I wanted to share my life's journey & experiences in depth with readers and sadhaks/seekers who are on a similar path so that they can get insight and more clarity on lot of issues which will deepen their faith and help them to see their own journey in a different light. The other reason of writing this book is to help other sadhaks/spiritual seekers gain insight and learn from my experiences. I never intended to write this book for any name or fame or money but rather my main intention is to help other seekers on their spiritual path so that they can purify their inner selves and experience higher states of consciousness, inner peace and inner freedom.

CONTENTS

Part A. More clarity on various spiritual topics based on my personal experiences of last twenty years

1. How to manifest your desires or turn your desires into reality?

The first step to manifest your desires is to release all your fears, doubts and all other negative thoughts or emotions which are blocking your way to success. Absolute faith is required to manifest and fear energy weakens your faith. Fear and faith can never go together. Where there is fear and doubt, there is no faith and where there is faith, there is no fear or doubt of any kind. So the first step is to release all your doubts, fears and all other negative elements through some form of release process/method/meditation/sadhna. To know more in detail about release sadhna/meditation you can read my article on release sadhna.

The second step is to do the process of forgiveness, which you do mentally. You forgive all those who have hurt you in your entire life so that you may release all your anger, hatred and pain against them, and then ask for forgiveness from all those whom you have hurt consciously or unconsciously, so that they can release all their anger, hatred and pain against you. It is upto you, if you want to ask forgiveness directly or want to do it just mentally.

The third step is of gratitude, unconditional love and divine cosmic energy, which is the energy/vibration/frequency of creation/manifestation. Divine cosmic energy can be directly invoked or received from the infinite, formless, divine cosmic dimension by connecting with it or you can invoke or receive it from your guru or any form of god you worship. In this third step you begin with a feeling of gratitude in your heart for all that you have received physically, materially, emotionally, mentally and spiritually in your entire life. You feel, imagine and visualize that unconditional love energy is continuously flowing from your heart (anahat chakra) and both your hands. You also feel, imagine and visualize that divine cosmic energy is continuously flowing from the point just above your head (crown/sahastrar chakra) . Then send unconditional love energy from your heart to everyone you know in your life, your family, friends, colleagues etc. Then send this unconditional love energy and divine cosmic energy to the whole of planet earth, whole of universe. Then finally send this love energy and divine cosmic energy to the place or person you need to heal or send it to the situation or outcome you want to manifest. You have to imagine or visualize this situation or outcome in your mind. But please make sure that whatever you manifest should not be against the free will of any person or should not interfere with the free will of any person.

2. How to make a choice or decision in your life?

* Whenever you make a choice or decision about anything in your life, just ask yourself what are the reasons behind making that particular choice or decision. Make a list of all the possible reasons.

* If the reasons are based on any kind of fear, guilt or any other negative thought or emotion, it's a wrong choice or wrong path/direction that you are planning to undertake. If the reasons are based on inner freedom, love, peace, happiness or positive thoughts or emotions, it is a right choice.

* If all your choices are based on negative emotions like fear or guilt, then first try to release your negative thoughts and emotions through your sadhana/meditation & then make a decision. Or for example, if one path/choice is based on fear and the other choice based on peace, happiness & inner freedom then first release the fear behind the first path/choice through your sadhna/meditation. Then reconsider both the paths again and make your final decision.

Till the time one reaches the state of Buddha which is a state of no mind or moksha, till then the mind needs a goal, a direction to focus on.

3. The importance of prayer before sadhna or meditation

After talking to a few seekers and sadhaks, I noticed that most of you don't pray before your sadhna/meditation. Here I am not talking about invocation but your personal prayer specifying what you want from your sadhna/meditation. It is very important that you know and ask for what you exactly want. You need to pray every time you sit for your sadhna/ meditation not just once or twice. For example, you want a specific healing or release of negative karma or purification etc. Based on what you want, Lord Shiva (supreme, static & pure consciousness) will give you the wisdom, clarity and direction, while Shakti (supreme, pure and dynamic energy) will do the work of cleansing, healing, purification, manifestation, etc. The more intense & deep your prayer, the more intense & deep will be your sadhna/meditation. If you leave it on the guru or god (shiv & shakti) to decide for you, then know one thing for sure, that guru or god will only want the best & ultimate for you, so if you are not ready for the ultimate right now, then specify clearly and ask for what you want right now, not about what you want in future.

Doing any form of sadhna/meditation without the prayer will become directionless, whether it is release sadhna or mantra sadhna. Till the time you tell very clearly, god or guru will not know whether you want a specific healing or release of negative karma (negative thoughts or emotions, etc) or purification or some other specific desire that you want to be fulfilled. So doing a specific prayer every time before you begin your sadhna will give you better results in your sadhna. It does not matter if you repeat the same prayer everytime.

There is one type of prayer where you simply ask "Give me this or that" and there is another type of prayer where you ask for release of your blocks and negative karma, cleansing and purification of your inner being which is coming in the way of getting what you want. Once you remove these blocks and obstacles and work towards your inner purification, you will get what you want. That is why release sadhna/meditation and forgiveness, gratitude and unconditional love sadhna/meditation are also very important along with your mantra sadhna/meditation.

But also remember one thing that if your prayers are not being answered the way you wanted it to, then you need to understand and realize that whatever is happening is happening for your best and ultimate good because god and guru will only want the best for you. Apart from this, one more thing you need to keep in mind, that you can pray for yourself, but while praying for others you need to know and find out if others also want exactly what you are praying for. Because if they don't want what you are praying for, then it will interfere with their free will and that is not right. We should never interfere with the free will of any person.

4. More clarity on unconditional love and acceptance

Unconditional love means giving love unconditionally without any terms & conditions or expectations, but unconditional love and acceptance does not mean that you become a doormat and let people take advantage of you and use you. It only means that you don't hold anything negative like anger or hate, etc in your heart against anyone, and are able to let go and forgive. But at the same time, you need to be strong and firm and not let anyone use you or take advantage of you. Allowing people to use you and take advantage of you or hurt you or harm you will only encourage them and give them strength to do more & more and will also enhance their ego. And you will be responsible to a great extent for not stopping them and encouraging them & making their ego even bigger. So a victim is a victim because they are allowing people to victimize them, hence they have no right to blame others but themselves for it.

Accepting yourself and others (the way they are & the way you are) does not mean that there is no need to change or grow or improve further, rather accepting the good and bad in you and others is only the first step. The next step is to work on your weaknesses and purify yourself, release the negative aspects within you and learn the lessons you need to learn on your spiritual path. As far as others are concerned, you also need to make them realize their weaknesses and negative aspects in a positive way, if they are not realizing on their own but there is always a possibility that they may or may not realize . This will depend on how much surrender and faith they have in you. If they do not realize or understand what you are telling them, you just accept the outcome and move on.

Accepting life the way it is means that you are allowing the past karma (kriyaman, sanchit and prarabdha) to dominate your life and control your destiny but in order to change the course of your destiny you need to release and erase the past sanchit karma through your sadhna and create a new destiny. If everyone accepts everything the way it is, then there will be no growth or change in life. For example, if Gandhiji and other freedom fighters had accepted everything the way it was, and given unconditional love to the Britishers, allowing them to take advantage of Indians, then they would have only encouraged the Britishers to do more of what they were already doing and enhanced their egos and they would have never made any effort to work towards freedom and change. So it is very important to understand through this example that there is no need to hold on to any anger or fear or hatred against the victimizers, rather it is important to release all the negativity against them & forgive them in order to have a clear and stable mind, but at the same time you need to be strong, firm and positive to find a way to stop people who are victimizing and taking advantage of you. And while you are doing this, you can send unconditional love energy to them indirectly from the distance (mentally during your sadhna/meditation) to resolve the unresolved issues of the past and dissolve negative energy and sanchit karma. Avoid doing it directly, otherwise it will appear as if you are trying to please them (their egos) and it will only make matters worse.

5. Release sadhna/meditation

This sadhna/dhyan is only for people who are initiated in any form of divine cosmic energy. You can also invoke divine cosmic energy from the infinite cosmic dimension by connecting with it. People who are deep believers of any deity (devi or devata/god or goddess) or are deeply connected to any ishta/deity, or have deep faith and devotion towards them, can invoke the divine energies of their ishta/deity by praying to them. Here the release sadhna/meditation is not only about the past life karmic release but the release of all the karma of this life also which is deeply embedded in your subconscious and unconscious mind in the form of negative incidents, memories, psychic impressions, conditionings, emotions (anger, hate, fear, jealousy, greed, sadness, pain, hurt, etc). Here we are only talking about kriyaman and sanchit karma.

RELEASE PROCESS

STEP ONE: Invoke the divine energy/shakti of any form of god you believe in or have faith in. You can also invoke divine cosmic energy/shakti of formless dimension of god/goddess. You pray to your guru and god to guide you, help you, and protect you during the release. You can be specific about the release in your prayer– for example, you can say "Help me to release this anger, this guilt, this fear, this pain, this sadness, etc". If you chant any form of mantra regularly, then you can play that mantra cd in the background with low sound. If you don't practice any mantra sadhna then no need to play any mantra cd and you can go to the next step.

STEP TWO: Start inhaling and exhaling deeply, intensely and slowly for 2-5 minutes without thinking about anything. This is dynamic breathing so there is no need to hold the breath between exhalations and inhalations. And there should not be any gap between inhalation and exhalation, which means that the moment inhalation ends, exhalation should start and vice versa.

STEP THREE: If there is something already on the surface to be released, then work on it immediately or allow your consciousness to go into your past events or simply remember the incidents from the time you were born up to now and let the negative events come to the surface to be released.

With each in- breath, visualize the negative situation & feel the negative emotion- the anger, pain, fear, etc, and with each out-breath consciously let go and release the energy of negative emotion, thought, or negative psychic impression. Don't hold your breath and don't take breaks between the inhalation and exhalation. It may happen that after sometime on its own the breathing may take its own rhythm which means that it might become more intense or fast or more slower and deeper, so whatever happens just let it happen and flow with the rhythm. Otherwise you just continue to do deep & slow inhalation and exhalation. Sometimes if there is very heavy karma coming on the surface to be released, the breathing may become very intense, fast & rapid. In that case you just go with the flow. This is a release process at the physical body (annamaya kosha) level but there is another way of release which is at the mind body level (manomaya kosha) which is more subtle in nature.

MENTAL RELEASE PROCESS: In mental release process, you imagine the incident of the past and then imagine or visualize yourself acting out with the same intensity the way you had wanted to but could not do it in the past and it remained suppressed in your subconscious mind. For instance, in the past you wanted to express your anger or slap somebody, but you could not do it or you wanted to say something and you could not say it. Then you can imagine yourself doing it mentally and in the process you will be releasing it mentally. The same technique can be used for other suppressed psychic impressions and emotions. When the release happens at the mind body level (manomaya kosha) then there is no need to concentrate on the breathing; it will happen on its own.

TIME DURATION FOR RELEASE: The minimum time period for this release process is 30 minutes and the maximum can be any length of time you feel comfortable with. You need to release till all your negative impressions, thoughts and emotions related to that particular incident or situation are completely released. It may happen in one session or multiple sessions. To know and test if you have completely released it or not, you need to remember or imagine the same situation or incident of the past and if you don't feel anything negative regarding it, rather you feel peaceful or neutral or not affected, then you have truly released it but if there is even little negative feeling still left in you, then you need to do more release on that particular issue.

RELEASE THROUGH FORGIVENESS: Another way of release and purification is through forgiveness where you forgive others and ask for forgiveness from others. If you are able to truly forgive then a huge amount of karma (all your anger, pain, etc) will be released instantly and you will feel very light.

RELEASING ON BEHALF OF OTHERS: You can also release the anger, pain, hurt, etc of other people if you can feel what they are feeling, within you, through the same process. This usually happens when you have achieved a state of oneness or you are operating at the level of universal mind.

STEP FOUR: In the end, thank god, your guru and divine cosmic energy/shakti for all the release and purification.

STEP FIVE: After every release session, you may feel little tired, hungry or drained out, so you should do a meditation to relax your mind and body or do love & gratitude meditation to fill the empty space (that you have created within you after throwing all the garbage out) with the positive energy of love and gratitude. It will re energize your entire being.

6. Man hi karta, man hi bhogta (mind is the doer, mind is the experiencer). Negative & positive belief systems

All the negative & positive conditionings and belief systems (negative/positive thought + negative/positive emotion + negative/positive psychic impression or memory) are very deeply rooted within us, as my guru says, "man hi karta, man hi bhogta" (mind is the doer and mind is the experiencer). With the help of sadhna/meditation and contemplation, we need to start erasing or letting go of the negative belief systems first and then finally even release the positive ones so that we are free from the impact of all these belief systems & be able to activate our atma shakti from within. This will strengthen our faith & we will be able to listen to the voice of the atma or guru within us.

If there are people around us who have stronger belief systems (positive or negative), then they will overpower our mind with it. On the other hand if our belief systems are equally or more stronger than theirs, then we will be able to stop them from overpowering our mind. These are mind power games that people play on each other (consciously or unconsciously), but the power and faith that comes from atma shakti (higher and more subtle divine energy) is beyond all this.

For example if somebody curses you and you accept it as your belief system, then it will materialize but if you reject it and have faith coming from your atma and your guru (guru consciousness) that nothing wrong will happen to you, then this positive energy will materialize.

Another example would be, if you believe, you have committed a sin and you will suffer for it, then this will materialize sooner or later (in this life or next life), on the other hand if you believe that you have done nothing wrong so there is no need to suffer for it, it will eventually materialize, and you will not suffer for it. Guilt comes from different belief systems existing in your mind. Everything you believe as good, bad, right, wrong is a belief system within the confines of the mind. For example, if you believe that ghosts, spirits, entities and demons are more powerful than you then this belief will materialize when you have such an experience. But if you have faith (which is infinitely more powerful) and you believe that the power of the god or supreme is the ultimate power and everything negative can dematerialize and dissolve in its presence, then this will become your reality.

But that does not mean that you can go against the laws of the universe or spiritual laws or laws of karma. For example, if you do anything against the free will of anyone and believe that nothing will happen to you is wrong, because the truth is that you will have to face the consequences of it, since the law of karma is beyond the dimension of your mind and it works whether you believe in it or not.

For example, if you force an adult to do something against his or her wish, who has a mind of its own and a free will, then it is against the spiritual law and you will face the karmic consequences. Another example would be when anyone hurts or harms someone with a bad intention of taking revenge. There can be many examples like these so it is very important to have clarity that whether what you are facing is the result of your negative belief or conditioning or is it the result of your negative karma or is it a result of your going against the laws of nature, universe & spirit. This can be known only through intuition & by understanding the spiritual and universal laws. Once the mind is pure and free from all good and bad conditionings, it will automatically flow according to the laws of nature, universe and soul.

Never have belief systems that strengthen your ego even though they superficially appear quite positive, for example when you say that "I am more powerful than others, I can heal anybody, I can predict future", etc. Rather than saying or believing "I am the doer", "I can do it", have faith and say, "It will happen through the grace of god, if I give my 100% effort, as my mind and body is only a medium to do gods work".

It's not easy to get rid of all negative belief systems (negative thought + negative emotion + negative psychic impression) because they are very deeply rooted in your subconscious and unconscious, so you need the grace of your guru, strength from your soul, along with your release sadhna/meditation, forgiveness, gratitude and unconditional love sadhna/ meditation to release all these negative blocks, conditionings and belief systems. Converting negative belief systems into positive ones is not enough because positive belief systems, if not strong will not be able to hold itself for very long, and especially if your atma shakti is weak, your mind will have an upper hand, will overpower you and trick you into again going back to your negative believe systems. To retain your positive strength and generate pure faith, you need to awaken your atma shakti which will give you the positive strength to deal with your negative beliefs and finally transform them permanently into positive ones.

But just having positive strength, attitude or belief is not enough, you also need to work hard and acquire the skills required to achieve your goals. For example if you want to become a good badminton player, then along with your positive belief system you need to work hard to acquire the skills required to become a good badminton player. So in short we can say that positive belief system + hard work + grace of guru or atma helps you to get what you want. People who have faith (coming from their atma/soul) need not worry about positive or negative belief systems because faith is infinitely more powerful than your belief systems. True faith is always unshaken while belief systems are. So absolute faith and hard work will help you achieve what you want. But to acquire this unshaken faith one must do sadhna/meditation and seva/selfless work to purify their mind and heart. In other words through inner purification and cleansing, you will receive guru's or god's grace and your atma shakti & faith will strengthen. Atma shakti gets awakened through your sadhna/meditation, seva/selfless work, bhakti/devotion, faith and surrender and guru's or gods grace.

The day your mind is free from all the good & bad belief systems and conditionings of the past, present & future, then your mind consciousness(chetna) will merge with higher consciousness(atma) and you will attain true wisdom and clarity & then whatever you want will materialize instantly.

7. The root cause of everything is your ego

The root cause of everything is your ego (mind and body) or simply "I" (an identity created through this mind and body).

Kam, krodh, lobh, moh comes from ego.

Ego is this small "I am" or your very small limited identity and personality with your name, position, likes, dislikes etc (all your thoughts, emotions, feelings, actions, desires).

One needs to use this ego as a tool to play the drama of life but not get attached to this ego or identity. The only wall between you & god is this wall of false self/ego/identity.

Surrender & faith to a guru means that you surrender your false self/ego to him so that he can start his work of destroying & finishing your ego, so that you can (your soul) be free again & be one with god forever.

If you do not give your ego/false self to your guru completely, with absolute faith then it's not possible for your guru to do his main work, which is to dissolve this ego/identity completely. Guru can also help you to raise your level of consciousness so that you can consciously watch your ego and detach yourself from it so that the process of death of ego becomes less painful for you.

Ego has a free will & the guru cannot go against it.

There is only one major fear which is the fear of death of ego/self/ identity. Every other fear comes from this fear. Rather every other emotion comes from this fear of death. Fear is an indication that your ego is about to die but your ego does not want to die. If there is more ego, there will be more fear and vice versa.

Don't become a victim or victimizer. Don't let people dominate you & do not dominate others, because both ways you let the ego become strong. Nobody is telling you to react and make more karma for yourself but you need to act with wisdom and not let others misuse your ego and take advantage of it. For example, if you dont act when a thief comes to your house, then you will in a way encourage that thief to do more and more thefts. You must learn to use your ego as a tool to play the drama of life well, without reacting but acting firmly when required as Lord Krishna did. If in case you react negatively, then you must immediately release that negative energy through release sadhna/meditation along with unconditional love sadhna/meditation to avoid creating more karma for yourself.

If you have spiritual strength within you –you can stop others from dominating you, controlling you & at the same time you will also not have any need to control or dominate others. In case of children you can use your ego with detachment to discipline and train their minds.

The more you (your ego) depend on others for your physical, mental, emotional & spiritual needs, the more power they will have to control you or dominate you or manipulate you. So only depend on your guru and god (the supreme almighty, the ultimate one, shiv & shakti/purush & prakriti/divine mother & father) for all your needs and be sure that it will be taken care of, unconditionally for you, if you have absolute faith and surrender in them.

8. Who is a true yogi or yogini?

A true yogi or yogini is not the one who pretends to renounce everything externally while internally still crave and desire or have attachments, but a true yogi or yogini is the one who may or may not renounce anything externally but he or she will definitely renounce everything internally with total detachment towards everyone and everything.

Just by wearing orange robes and rudraksha mala will not make you a true yogi, when internally you are even attached to your robe and the mala you wear, whereas on the other hand the one who may externally wear beautiful clothes or jewellery but internally is totally detached to what he or she is wearing is a true yogi. Similarly a true yogi may be living in a big mansion but will be totally detached towards it internally, which means that if he is asked to leave his mansion or if it is destroyed, it will not bother or affect him. On the other hand a false yogi living in a simple hut, may get deeply bothered if he is asked to leave or if his hut is destroyed.

A true yogi or yogini is totally fearless and is not affected by the opinions, views or perceptions of the outside world or society.

A true yogi or yogini is not affected by praise or criticism by others internally though on the outside he or she may act differently, on the other hand a false yogi may pretend to be not affected by anything on the outside but is actually deeply affected on the inside (in his mind).

A true yogi or yogini may have all kinds of relationships in the outside world but will be totally detached towards them on the inside which may include his wife or husband, girlfriend or boyfriend, sister or brother, children or parents. Whereas a false yogi may renounce every relationship on the outside but may still be deeply attached to them internally. For example a false yogi may not be able to even imagine and visualize the death of his family, friends, etc in his mind because he still not free from his attachments.

A true yogi is the one who neither suppresses anything nor overindulges in anything. Everything happens in moderation with no extremes. He is neither for nor against anything. He has no attraction or repulsion towards anything including life or death.

That is why my guru says that you can achieve everything being in the family and in the world, so there is no need to renounce anything externally or go to the Himalayas but do sadhna/meditation and purify your mind so that you can renounce everything at the level of your mind which is within you not outside you.

9. Karma = Mind = Maya

One simple step can liberate you from the so called maya jaal or the clutches of maya. We are born enlightened and freedom is our birthright. We only need to get conscious of our enlightened being. This can happen in just one single step. You must be wondering how is it possible.

Everything is possible provided you are open and receptive to it. So are you ready to expand your consciousness and go beyond the limitations of your mind? If your answer is yes then let's explore and understand what is Karma, Mind & Maya, first separately and then explore the dimension of how are they one and not separate which means Karma = Mind = Maya

What is Mind?

Your mind is all your positive and negative thoughts and emotions which create positive or negative (good or bad) conditioning/patterns/behavior/desires. Your every thought is a form of energy or conditioning or impression creating your own unique destiny or path. You are only aware of your conscious mind but still unaware of your subconscious and unconscious mind which is the store house of all your thoughts, emotions, desires, impressions and conditioning's. Since you are not aware of this part of your mind, you have no control over it. In other words you have no control over your destiny or prarabdha karma. To have the control to change or recreate your destiny, you have to first awaken your subconscious (dream state) and unconscious (sleep state) and be in total awareness of your subconscious and unconscious mind. Then use some tools like meditation, dhyan, sadhna & seva (selfless activity) to do the purification of your mind and body and in the process release and dissolve the negative sanchit karma (your thoughts, emotions, desires and impressions) & recreate your destiny.

What is Karma?

Your karma is all your accumulated negative and positive thoughts, emotions, memories, psychic impressions & desires. Your good karma is your positive thoughts, emotions, desires, mind conditioning & impressions & visa verse. Now you must do a lot of self introspection and be conscious of your good & bad karma that you have accumulated over lifetimes. How you react to all the situations and circumstances occurring in your life including the behavior of people towards you is a result of your own karma. So in other words whether you react negatively or positively towards a situation or a person is the result of your sanchit and prarabdha karma. If you change the reaction, you change the karmic pattern and if after your sadhna/meditation and inner purification no reaction (good or bad) happens within you and you are neutral and peaceful, not reacting in the given situation, then you have cleared all your karma towards that situation or person. It's high time that one must stop blaming the outside situations or people or the world in general and start taking some actions towards changing their inside through various means of inner cleansing and self purification. (To know more about karma you can read the article on theory of karma)

What is Maya?

Maya is the dual nature of the mind which includes the good and bad conditioning of the mind, the positive and negative thoughts and emotions leading you to a positive or negative destiny or future. It is the sense of illusion created by your ego which is the outcome of all your gross & subtle bodies and mind together and gives you the feeling that you are separate from everyone or everything. When the ego (mind and subtle body) dissolves completely, then it is the end of this maya and duality and beginning of oneness within you. This is when you and the almighty become one in all its dimensions of form and formless from the gross to the subtle.

What is Moksha or Liberation?

When there are no positive or negative thoughts, emotions, desires or conditioning's that can overpower you, bind you or hold you in its clutches. When you go beyond the dimensions of mind or karma or maya, when there is no experience left, you become free and liberated. You then become pure consciousness or in other words you have arrived home! Arriving home is still not complete freedom or liberation as you no doubt are free from the clutches of mind but not from clutches of your body. For ultimate liberation or moksha or nirvana you need to be completely detached and free from your body also. Once you have reached the stage where you have gone beyond the mind and body both, when mind and body cannot overpower you anymore, which means your mind and body can no longer cause any pain or suffering to your being or in other words when you are no longer affected by the pain and suffering of the mind and body both, then it means that all your karma is finished/dissolved or worked out and now your being is able to acquire a will to leave its mind and body when it wishes to or rather when the divine wishes to, as you no longer exist now, only the supreme exists, then you finally attain your final nirvana which is called by buddha as Mahaparinirvana.

10. Enlightenment to liberation

Meaning of enlightenment: When I use the word spiritual enlightenment, it only means the enlightenment or awakening of the mind to its full potential. In this state your limited mind or ego (I) expands to infinity. In this state your consciousness can experience the very high states of extreme joy & happiness, ecstasy of the mind on your spiritual path. This is the stage of agya chakra when the kundalini shakti/energy reaches the third eye, where you experience yourself (your mind) to be infinite and feel your presence everywhere & in everything. This is the state of "Aham Brahmasmi" or "I am that I am" where you are able to see the whole brahmand/cosmos, all the dimensions within your mind. This is also a state where you get all mind powers or siddhies & can travel to any dimension you want to. This is a state where you feel one with everyone and everything. In this state you can experience and sense what others are feeling and thinking about you or in general. This will be a state of self-realization/soul-realization when you are in this state all the time and the kundalini shakti/energy is permanently residing at the agya chakra, but if you have some karma left at the lower dimensions then the shakti/energy has to leave this state and move downwards and will keep moving up and down till it dissolves all the karma's (all thoughts, emotions, desires, psychic impressions and memories). The state of self realization/soul realization is not moksha/nirvana because the infinite self/infinite mind/infinite ego still exists. In this state you are still not free from this mind or ego, therefore still not liberated. This state is only the beginning of living your life to its full potential & having higher and more subtle experiences, which are only states of the awakened or enlightened mind or higher subtle universal mind.

Your consciousness has to experience both life & death to its full potential to go beyond both, and get final liberation or nirvana.

You experience life to its full potential when the mind gets enlightened & awakened to its full potential & you will experience death to its full potential when your so called enlightened (infinite) mind or ego dissolves completely through the process of death. This is known as the art of dying.

When the mind or ego dissolves, all the experiences end with it. This happens when the kundalini shakti/energy reaches sahastrar chakra. The mind & ego goes through the process of death. There is no experience and desire of any kind at this point, even the desire to help others is not there. There is no happiness, no sadness, no love, no hate, and no compassion. There is simply nothing (no thought, no emotion, no feeling, no desire, no I, no dimension, no cosmos, no form, no images, no existence). What is now left is the state of pure consciousness clearly reflected in the mirror of nothingness. One can experience absolute silence and stillness in this infinite ocean of nothingness. This happens when the kundalini shakti/energy permanently finds its abode at sahastrar chakra. This is when you are finally liberated, free or attained the state of jeevanmukt or moksha. The physical body may or may not survive after this, but if it exists, it will exit only due to the prarabdh karma of the physical body which is still left. The body will now only be used to fulfill a divine purpose. Your final liberation or mahaparinirvana will only happen when all your prarabdh karma dissolves or finishes. Till then you will still be tied to your body and will go through the sufferings of the body.

But to reach this spiritual state where shakti/energy merges with shiva/consciousness and becomes static, you have to experience yourself as pure consciousness where there is nothing to be experienced but only the experiencer left, where there is nothing to be observed but only the observer left. In this state even the experience of nothingness is not there, what is left is the experiencer or simply pure consciousness or pure awareness. Here there is no individual or universal "I" left as "experiencer" but only pure awareness/pure being/pure consciousness!

11. Raise your level of consciousness

To awaken the Shiv within you, it is important to raise your level of consciousness because Shiv is nothing else but supreme and pure consciousness. It is always better to awaken the Shiv first before you awaken the Shakti/Kundalini Energy so that Shiv/Supreme Consciousness within you can control and take care of the Shakti/Energy once it is awakened.

First and foremost pray to Shiv/Supreme Consciousness and your guru to raise your level of consciousness and also to get more wisdom and clarity on your spiritual path. Secondly do Shiv mantra or guru mantra sadhna/meditation everyday, which means mentally chanting the mantra every day. Thirdly practice witnessing, watching or awareness. To practice this you must watch or witness or be aware of yourself the whole day. Watch/witness and be aware of your intentions, thoughts, emotions, desires, feelings, ego & attachments. Watch and witness all your actions with detachment like you watch a movie in the theatre. In other words be conscious and aware of yourself within you and outside you all the time. This will help to reduce your unconscious behaviour and will help you to act more consciously thereby raising your level of consciousness.

12. How do you know if you are ready for self realization or moksha?

The points listed below will tell you if you are ready for self realization or moksha or if you are simply fooling yourself.

1. If you are ready, you will have no other desire or need left to be fulfilled.

2. If you are ready for it, you will be completely detached from everything and every person in your life, (whether they are there with you or not, it will not bother or affect you in any way)

3. You will not need or require any company; rather you would be able to spend a lot of time alone. You will not feel loneliness but rather you will enjoy your aloneness.

4. You will be ready to make any kind of effort to get there no matter how many obstacles and challenges come your way, you will be giving all your energy and time doing sadhna, seva and intense bhakti to achieve your goal.

5. You will give yourself completely, (your body, your mind, your heart, your soul), without getting distracted, with complete focus on your goal, only have one thought day and night till you get there. There will be nothing left to distract you from your goal.

6. It will be as if you can't live without it. You will be very desperate and intense about it just like somebody drowning trying to save himself, giving his everything (100%) in that moment, or a fish out of water desperately wanting some water to survive.

7. You will be already in a state where you would have gone beyond being good and bad, right and wrong, ready to go beyond this duality of happiness and sadness, positivity and negativity, ready to acquire this neutral state where there is no

high and no low, there is only silence, only peace and absolute freedom.

8. You will be ready to die (here we are not talking about physical death, but death of your identity, your ego, your mind). Jab aap apne astitva ko puri tarike se samapta karne ke liye tayaar ho jaye. You will be ready to become nobody & nothing from being somebody & something. You will be ready to dissolve all your identities including your name, position, status (work and home both), for example you will be ready to dissolve your identity as a boss/doctor/engineer, identity as a father/mother, identity as a son/daughter, identity as a wife/husband, identity as a brother/sister, etc. You will be ready to dissolve, finish and let go everything that you have been and you currently are, till you are nothing or nobody. This does not mean leaving your family. It simply means getting detached from your own identity within you.

9. A person who is about to die will not care about anything (job, family, business, house car, etc) but he will have absolute faith that god will take care of everything once he or she is finished and dead (here again we are not talking of physical death but death of your identity, your astitva)

10. A person who is ready for death and is about to die will not worry about accumulating good or bad karma.

11. You will be fearless and not bothered about what people say and think of you as you continue to pursue your goal.

12. Last but not the least you will have complete surrender and faith in your guru and the supreme almighty.

13. More clarity on freedom or liberation

If you are or rather your "I" is on the spiritual path to gain something (to get some spiritual experiences, to get some powers or siddhies, etc) or have desire to become something (to become god, to become guru or to become somebody great, etc) then you are after lower or other spiritual goals, not moksha or liberation or self realization.

But if you are truly after liberation or moksha or self realization then there is actually nothing to achieve but on the other hand you need to let go of everything that you have accumulated till now. You need to be ready to lose everything including yourself (your identity). There should be no desire left in your "I" to become anything or anybody.

You need to do sadhna/meditation not to gain anything but rather to release everything and to empty or silence your mind.

When you say "I want liberation", then the saying itself is wrong because the problem here is "I" itself. The day your mind becomes empty & intellect becomes pure, you are then free from the small "I" which was operating at the level of the mind & intellect, but the big "I" operating at the level of soul, god or cosmos is still there and is creating duality. For example when you say "I am the soul" or when you say "I am Shiv" or when you say "aham bhramasmi", there is still duality. The day your "I" dies and you dissolve in the ocean of nothingness, then what is left or rather what emerges from within you (which has always been there & you were unable to see it because of your mind and your "I") is supreme and pure consciousness, energy and being.

14. How does ego or individual identity operate in the life of a liberated soul?

A liberated soul is an infinite ocean of supreme and pure consciousness & becomes a wave in the outside world when he or she needs to interact or teach or act with total consciousness & merges back in the still and silent ocean of nothingness, in an instant when no action is required.

Even while he is acting as a wave in the external world, deep within, he is always experiencing himself as the silent peaceful ocean.

The ocean is supreme consciousness or shiva which is absolute silence, peace, & stillness & the wave is created when the shiva/supreme consciousness merges with shakti/supreme energy and uses shakti (dynamic creative force) to create, to interact, to teach, to guide, or simply act. So there is no ego or individual identity for a liberated soul, but there is only the play of shiva/supreme consciousness and shakti/supreme energy through his mind and body.

15. Awaken the Buddha/Christ/Kalki within

We all in the past have heard about the shift which was going to happen in December 2012 when the earth frequencies were going to change and it would move from third dimension to fourth dimension. This shift was supposed to continue from 2012 to 2029. We also heard people say that Kalki, Christ, Buddha will come to save us and help us during this shift. If you all are waiting for one person to come and save us from all the suffering & disaster, then you can continue to wait and watch for another thousand years and nothing will happen while things will only get worse than ever.

It's high time we get up from the sleep and awaken ourselves. We all have to become Kalki's, Christ's & Buddha's for the shift and change to really happen. We need to awaken the powers within us and become as conscious as Christ was or Buddha was or Krishna was. This is what we refer to as Christ consciousness or Krishna consciousness or Buddha consciousness. Each one of us has to take the role of Christ, Krishna or Buddha because we are as powerful as they were. It is just a matter of realizing it and then believing in it. So let us stop depending on just one person and take collective responsibility for the positive change, the golden age or satyug that we are looking forward to!

16. Art of detachment or dying and de addiction

Process of detachment or dying : This is a process in which while doing release sadhna/meditation you visualize, imagine and witness the death of the person or imagine and witness the destruction or loss of an object that you want to get detached to (to know more on release sadhna/meditation you can read the article on release sadhna/meditation). And while imagining that you release the negative emotion of fear, pain, hurt, sadness, etc that comes on the surface. Remember all emotions, memories, psychic impressions, thoughts, are forms of energy which can be released and transmuted by divine cosmic energy and grace of the guru and god. To test your level of detachment you need to do this process again and witness your reaction. If there is still any negative reaction while doing this process then you need to release more till there is no reaction left and you feel peaceful, and you are no longer affected by it.

You can do the same process imagining or witnessing your own death to detach from your own body and mind & to create a distance from your mind & body.

Just doing this process once will not help if it is not intense so it has to be done a number of times till you feel no reaction occurring.

Also you need to test yourself by going to a secluded place for one month totally disconnected from the outside world and family with no mobile phone to see your level of detachment.

Process of detachment and de addiction : As we all know that attachment and addiction can be towards any person or thing. There are two types of attachments and addictions, one is positive and other is negative . Positive attachments are created due to holding positive and happy memories or psychic impressions, thoughts and emotions in our subconscious mind, unable to let go of it and vice versa. For example positive attachments will be due to getting attached to people for positive reasons like love, care, help, attention, respect etc, while negative attachments will be for negative reasons like hatred, jealousy, anger, pain, fear, sadness, etc. Besides this you can also get attached to things like house, car, clothes, jewelry, etc. Similarly both positive and negative addictions happen due to holding on to pleasurable memories, psychic impressions in our subconscious mind not wanting to let go of it rather having the desire to have more and more of it. For example positive addiction is getting addicted to something which is positive like exercising, cooking, working, cleaning, or getting addicted to people, etc while negative addiction is getting addicted to something negative like alcohol, smoking, drugs, etc. We have to understand that both positive attachment or addiction and negative attachment or addiction is not good. So in order to get rid of both positive and negative attachment and addiction we need to release all the good and bad memories, psychic impressions, feelings and thoughts through the release sadhna/meditation. If you will only release the bad memories, impressions, thoughts and feelings and not the good ones then you will only be free from the negative attachments but you will not be free from positive attachments and addictions. So in order to be free from your positive attachments and both your negative and positive addictions you must release all the good, pleasurable and happy memories, psychic impressions, thoughts and emotions also along with bad ones. (To know more about release sadhna/ meditation you can read my article on release sadhna/meditation).

17. Art of becoming fearless

It is very important that one should attain a state of fearlessness and absolute courage on the spiritual path to face the obstacles and challenges that come on the way. To attain this level of strength and courage one must be free from all kinds of fears.

In this process while doing release sadhna/meditation you need to mentally witness or imagine or visualize, the worst possible situation that can happen which generates fear in you and then release the negative emotion of fear, pain, etc. (To know more on release sadhna/meditation you can read the article on release sadhna). Remember emotions, memories, psychic impressions, thoughts, are forms of energy which can be released and transmuted by the cosmic divine energy and grace of the guru and god. The same process can be done for anger or any other emotion.

To test your level of fearlessness you need to go through the process again and witness your reaction. If there is still any negative reaction you need to release more till there is no reaction left and you feel peaceful, and you are no longer affected by it.

Just doing this process once will not help if it is not intense so it has to be done a number of times till you feel no reaction occurring. All kinds of fears majorly come from the fear of death so it is important that you release the fear of your own death and death or loss of others also.

Another way of overcoming your fears is by having complete and absolute faith in your guru and god, because where there is absolute and true faith there cannot be any fear, which is not easy for everyone to have.

18. What is true humility or humbleness?

Humility or humbleness coming from your ego is not true humility. When you (your ego) try or want to be humble and do the things like touching somebody's feet is just an egoic act not real humility. In fact true humbleness will never be there till you have an ego or you are attached or identified with your ego (your "I").

Note: To understand and know more about ego you can read chapters 2, 3 and 4 from the book "A New Earth" by Ekhart Tolle.

When your mind is completely purified and becomes empty and your ego (gross ego, subtle ego, infinite ego and cosmic ego) dissolves completely, or if you are able to completely detach yourself from your mind and ego, or if you are able to surrender your ego completely to your guru, then there will be no need to do anything else. To further give you more clarity on this issue, the truth is, that being humble or arrogant, both are an act of ego. Till you are something, whether humble or arrogant, you are operating at the level of ego. Ask yourself this question: Who is humble? And who is arrogant? Is it possible for your atma/soul to be either humble or arrogant? The answer is obviously no. Only your ego (I) can be either humble or arrogant because it is only the need of the ego to be something for its existence and survival. Only when you go beyond both humbleness and arrogance, and become nothing then you will be truly free from your ego, then you will be neither humble nor arrogant. You will simply be a pure being.

There are many people including sadhaks or seekers on this spiritual path who try to speak sweetly and softly or try to change their body language to show their humility but you can see their very subtle ego in that act. They are pretending or trying to be good because according to them being humble is being good. They are wearing a mask and hiding their real self.

Let me make one thing very clear to you that being good is as much an act of ego as being bad. When you say that I am good or I am bad: in both these sayings "I" is still there.

Ask yourself this simple question: Who is good? and Who is bad? because based on what I have experienced, atma (higher consciousness) is neither good nor bad. It is only the jeev atma (your mind and ego) which is either good or bad, who is using this mind and body to fulfill its desires and gain experiences to learn and grow and evolve. So from now on don't be mistaken by the fact that if you are good, you have no ego. All Tamsic, Rajsic and Satvic gunas (gross and subtle attributes or qualities) have ego. Only at the level of atma or parmatma you are free from all gunas or attributes or qualities whether good or bad. At the level of atma/soul you are no longer this or that, you no longer have this or have that, you no longer want this or want that, because in truth you then become nothing.

19. Dual nature of mind. How to go beyond it?

All of us have a mind which is dual in nature, which means it has both good and bad side or karma (good and bad thoughts, emotions, desires, qualities, attribute, characteristics, likes & dislikes, suppression & overindulgence) , etc. The more the ego, the more the mind is divided in two opposite extremes. Both the good and the bad side of the mind is not real, it is only created by the mind consciousness & energy to experience good & bad for its spiritual growth, learning and finally liberation. If you give too much importance to the good, your mind will pull you with the same intensity towards the bad. This is because good and bad are the two sides of the same coin, where the coin is your mind or ego. To go beyond this dual nature of the mind and to heal the divide in your mind, you need to go beyond both good and bad, praise and criticism, etc. Witness and watch the good and bad in your mind but don't get attached or identified with it. First release the bad from your mind and then finally release even the good.

There is another way to go beyond this duality, where you accept both good and bad equally and not complain about anything. Just continue to empty your mind from both good and bad through your sadhna/meditation. See and understand that it is nothing but a play of maya/illusion. Now imagine a play or movie without a villain. With no villain, the importance and value of hero also goes away, there is no juice left. It will now become very boring & dull as there cannot be any fight between hero and the villain. The good is created to win over bad but if there is no bad then what will be the need of the good and if both are not there, will there be need of any drama or fight ?. The purpose of this maya/illusion especially the fight between the good and bad is only meant for spiritual growth, evolution and learning. Both divine and devil are just a part of this play of maya or illusion and they are there for a purpose. You will value the good only when you see and experience the bad. For example you will give value to the hero when you see the villain or value the divine when you see the devil. The more you encounter the bad the more your intensity will increase to know and experience the good, and a time will soon come when you (your mind & ego) will get tired and bored of even the good and you will then want freedom from both. A state of oneness in spirituality can be achieved when you go beyond this duality of good and bad, and this is how your atma/soul is always in a state of oneness. This process requires a very high state of consciousness and awareness.

20. God is beyond both divine and devil

This is to give more clarity to people who fear the devil and assume divine to be god.

God is beyond both divine and devil. Divine and devil both are an important part of maya or illusion and duality, created by the supreme divine mother or shakti/supreme divine energy to reach god, to know god, to experience god and to be conscious of god.

Here I am referring divine as devta (good karma) and devil as asur (bad karma). Both divine and devil are created for shakti to merge with shiva or in other words the individual consciousness to merge with god consciousness. This happens when a strong urge is created within shakti or individual consciousness to move towards shiva or god consciousness.

This urge is created due to the struggle between the divine and devil forces within you, and outside you, and is created when you want to be free or want to go beyond this pain of struggle. This urge or intensity pushes the shakti or individual consciousness to move towards shiva or god consciousness.

Good and bad karma is created by interacting with both divine and devil forces within and outside you, to have a variety of good and bad experiences for optimum spiritual growth and learning. If you only have good experiences in your life, then your growth and learning will be very less and there is a danger of your ego becoming very big. If you only have bad experiences then also the growth will be less and the ego might take a victim identity, will blame others and not take responsibility of its actions.

If you are unconscious you will not use these opportunities of good and bad experiences for your growth and learning rather you will end up creating more good and bad karma for yourself which will lead to more good and bad experiences and this can go on endlessly till you become more conscious and aware and realize that you are chained in the web of your own karma. Only when you become more conscious and aware through your sadhna/meditation and the grace of guru or god, you are able to see all good and bad experiences as opportunities for learning and growth. Then you will be able to stop creating more karma for yourself and start releasing the past karma which was created unconsciously by you. That is why we can say that destiny can be created either unconsciously or consciously.

When you (your ego) go through the pain, trauma, suffering, fear, etc caused by the devil or asur forces, then your search for god begins, and when you reach a state of helplessness then you surrender yourself (your ego) to god or guru. So the role of devil is very important to reach god or realize god within you.

When you experience higher spiritual experiences with the help of devta or divine forces, your faith strengthens and you get the courage to move towards god consciousness. So the role of devta is equally important in realizing god and knowing the truth.

In some of the religious & spiritual books and traditions people have condemned & feared the devil and worshipped the divine/devta which has only increased the fight between divine and devil since both are egoistic. The time has come for us to realize the deeper truth and give our respect, gratitude and love to both the divine and the devil forces knowing and understanding that the real purpose of both is to help us learn, grow, evolve and finally merge with god. Only when we can do this we will be able to go beyond both divine and devil and finally merge with god consciousness. In my spiritual journey I have deeply and truly given respect, love and gratitude to both the divine and devil forces, and believe me I have got help from both to reach my goal. Shiva or god or guru will use the devil forces to create obstacles in your path and to pull you down to test your longing, faith, courage and intensity and in turn prepare you for your goal. Guru and god will use the divine forces to help you to get the strength to move towards your goal.

In other words either you accept praise and criticism, success and failure both or go beyond both. Just accepting one is not possible because if you (ego) will get affected by praise and success, you (ego) will also get equally affected by criticism and failure but if you truly go beyond praise and success and no longer get affected by it, then definitely you will not get affected by criticism and failure also. Similarly if you easily get carried away by the good experiences, then you will be easily and equally affected by the bad experiences also, so either accept both or go beyond both. Don't try to run away or escape or avoid either of them. You have come on this planet earth to experience and face it and go beyond it, not run away from it.

So God is neither divine nor devil but uses both divine and devil forces to play its leela/drama or fulfill its purpose. God is beyond both; God is simply nothing, just pure consciousness, pure energy. This is my realization and my experience.

21. Can one experience divine love on physical, mental, emotional and spiritual level?

This is to give more clarity to sadhaks/spiritual seekers who are married or in relationship with someone and they want to experience divine love in their relationships, provided both the partners are sadhaks or seekers on a spiritual path.

Can one experience divine love on physical, mental, emotional and spiritual level?

The answer is yes provided you are on a higher consciousness plane and operating from higher chakras (anahat/heart, vishuddhi/throat, agya/third eye and sahastrar/crown) and not from lower chakras (muladhar/root or base, swadhisthan/sex and manipur/navel)

Your perception, understanding and experience from higher chakras will be very different as compared to your perception, understanding and experience from your lower chakras.

For example when your energy and consciousness is at the swadhisthan/sex chakra, you will perceive, understand and experience only sexual feelings and energies, attachment and obsession but if your energy and consciousness is at anahat/heart chakra, you will perceive, understand and experience unconditional love (with no expectations and conditions) provided your anahat/heart chakra is opened, activated and purified. And when your energy and consciousness is at sahastrar /crown chakra, you will perceive, understand and experience divine love and oneness with no attachment of any kind, provided your sahastrar/crown chakra is opened, activated and purified.

When two partners make love to each other physically and their consciousness and energy is at the level of swadhisthan/sex chakra, their experience & perception will be only sexual with no experience of love but only that of attachment.

When both partners make love to each other physically and if their consciousness & energy is at the level of anahat/heart chakra, they will experience and perceive love and compassion with deeper understanding and gratitude towards each other.

When both partners make love to each other physically and if their consciousness and energy is at the level of sahastrar/crown chakra, they will experience and perceive each other as divine. They will experience divine love, bliss and oneness. Here their two separate individual ego identities will merge into god consciousness and become one with god consciousness and enter into a state of super consciousness or samadhi.

To raise your level of consciousness and energy to higher chakras while making love, or interacting physically with each other, both the partners should see their bodies as a temple of god and see each other as divine beings (as shiv and shakti), and not just as human beings. They should feel devotion, respect, gratitude and pure unattached love towards each other. Realizing and understanding that in truth they both are one, not two separate beings.

To constantly maintain your consciousness at higher levels you need to purify your mind and release attachments, negative thoughts and negative emotions through sadhna/meditation and seva/selfless work.

22. A self realized and enlightened master will not know everything

Have you ever heard any realized master, siddha, guru or saint saying that he or she knows everything? Realizing self or god or getting liberated is different from knowing everything. A realized soul may not have all the knowledge which a doctor or engineer or scientist has. He may not even have the knowledge of all the spiritual paths or yogic sciences. Someone who has attained realization through the path of karma yoga and bhakti yoga may or may not have the deep knowledge about the path of kriya yoga or kundalini yoga. For example, he may not be having knowledge of the yogic science behind levitation or other siddhies/powers.

Once you are one with the ultimate source whether you call it shoonya, nothingness, pure consciousness or energy, you lose your individual being or identity and there is no desire left within you to know anything. After that whatever knowledge is revealed to you is based on what god wants to reveal it to you for a divine purpose or a divine mission.

When you go to a realized guru, saint or master, you go with an intention to know and realize what he has realized and experienced himself, and not with the intention to acquire all kinds of knowledge and different meditation techniques.

Any realized master or siddha will have only that knowledge which he or she has acquired, realized and experienced during his or her spiritual journey towards ultimate truth. This is one reason why different forms of knowledge and meditation techniques or kriyas are imparted to people by different masters and saints for realizing the same truth.

23. More clarity on three most important spiritual states and the knowledge acquired.

Atma sakshatkar or atma anubhav or experience of your soul happens at the visshuddhi/throat chakra and this state can become permanent if kundalini shakti/energy and your consciousness remains at vishuddhi/throat chakra forever without moving down again. Here you will experience your soul which is higher energy & higher consciousness but you will not experience oneness with everyone and everything. Your individual identity will still remain intact. You may still have desires at this point and the need to acquire more knowledge may still be there. Here you will experience & realize your soul but you will still not know everything.

Self realization happens at agya/third eye chakra if shakti/energy and consciousness remains there forever without moving down. Here you experience a state of "aham brahmasmi" where you experience your oneness with the whole brahmand, the whole existence. In this state within you, you can experience what others are feeling and thinking. In other words you can read people's mind. At this stage if you still have desire to acquire more knowledge then you will intuitively receive from the ultimate source within you, provided it is for a divine purpose. But you will still not know everything. You can access only that knowledge from gyanmaya kosha (intellect body) which you have acquired in your past lives. At this stage if you have no desire left to know and acquire anything, then you will move towards liberation. The desire to gain more knowledge or powers or siddhies will not let you move towards sahastrar/crown chakra for liberation and ultimate truth, and your energy and consciousness will continue to remain at agya/third eye chakra.

Once the shakti/energy and consciousness reaches the sahastrar/crown chakra and resides there permanently then there is no desire left to know anything or acquire anything. Then even the SELF or AHAM dies or dissolves and what is left is shoonya, nothingness, pure & supreme consciousness, pure and supreme energy, pure & supreme wisdom or intelligence. In this state now everything happens according to the divine will. So whatever knowledge is revealed or not revealed will be also according to the divine will.

24. What you want for yourself, first learn to give it to others.

If there is anything less or lacking in your life, then for you to receive that first start giving it to others. This is a law of universe and law of karma that whatever you give, you get it back.

So if you want to receive unconditional love and respect, then first start giving it to others. The same goes with money, knowledge, freedom, help, etc. This is also one of the reasons why one should do seva/selfless work.

It is a spiritual law that everyone must donate or share 20 % of their income with others. If this is truly practiced you will never have any financial problems in your life.

People who have problem in giving anything or cannot give that easily and make all kinds of excuses for not giving or sharing anything, are people whose anahat/heart chakra is still not open, activated and purified, and their energy/shakti and consciousness is residing in lower chakras, so these people need to do more sadhna/meditation and seva (purification of heart and mind through release sadhna/meditation & forgiveness, gratitude and unconditional love sadhna/meditation).

This is for you to know and learn the spiritual laws and to make you understand the importance of giving.

25. Use your wisdom & intuition to know what to read & what to avoid on the spiritual path.

Use your wisdom or pray to your guru and god to give you enough wisdom to know which spiritual books or articles to read and which to avoid. If you read something which leads to more doubt and confusion then let go of that information. Whatever you choose to read should give you more clarity on your spiritual path, so be very selective in what you read. Unnecessary information will lead to unnecessary thinking which will be a waste your time and energy. Your perception and understanding depends or is based on the level of your inner purification and your consciousness. Impure mind and ego will distort information. As my guru says that if you are wearing blue goggles, you will see and perceive everything as blue. Your mind needs to be completely empty, clean & egoless to perceive and know the truth reflected in what you read and see. As you become more and more pure and conscious, you are able to deeply understand and realize that knowledge also which you were unable to do in the past. Even if you are impure and unconscious, sometimes with the grace of guru and god, you get sudden clarity and realization which raises your level of consciousness and purifies you further. But this will happen only if you have faith and surrender towards your guru and god. Don't share books and articles with others which may lead to more confusion. The books and articles you share with others should be the ones which will give them more clarity and understanding. True knowledge, understanding & realization comes from true and real experience so wait till you experience it yourself.

Also avoid analyzing experiences in your sadhna or spiritual path because you may be very impure to understand and realize the true and deeper meaning hidden within it. In those very few moments when your mind is clear and empty even though for a short while, you may have intuitive flashes which will give you immediate and sudden realizations and understandings which will come from a space beyond your mind. Rely more on your intuition & wisdom than your mind. Real intuition & wisdom happens when the mind is clear and empty, not when mind is full of thoughts or emotions. When you respond to a given situation according to your wisdom and intuition, which is beyond logic and emotions, it is perfect (neither right, nor wrong). This is what we call as conscious acting not unconscious reacting.

The reading material that you can keep with you, which helped me and which can help you in your spiritual journey is:-

1. Light on the guru and disciple relationship by Swami Satyananda Saraswati from Bihar school of yoga

2. Life's Mysteries by Osho.

3. 2nd, 3rd & 4th chapters on ego from the book A New Earth by Ekhart Tolle. You can also keep and read Stillness Speaks by Ekhart Tolle, which will help you to experience few moments of stillness.

4. Kundalini Tantra By Swami Satyananda Saraswati to know about shakti or kundalini sadhna.

5. Samkhya Darshan: Yogic Perspective on Theories of Realism by Swami Niranjanananda Saraswati

Samkhya is one of the earliest schools of Indian philosophy and most systems, including yoga, have been drawn from or influenced by it. Samkhya is a dualistic philosophy and postulates two eternal realities: Purusha, the witnessing consciousness, and Prakriti, the root cause of creation, composed of the three gunas.

This text highlights the unique contribution of Samkhya philosophy in man's quest to understand his true nature. It discusses the practical theories of causation, manifestation, bondage and liberation.

For the spiritual aspirant, Samkhya is the metaphysics of self-realization and yoga is the sadhana or means to achieve it. Samkhya Darshan contains the full Sanskrit text of Ishvara Krishna's Samkhya Karika as well as transliteration and translation.

26. True love is beyond ego, attachment and expectations

It is not possible to experience true love in any relationship where there is ego, attachment and expectations or conditions on either side. The more the ego, attachment and expectations, the more will be the conflict and pain in any relationship.

True love happens where there is freedom, purity and awareness, where there is no possessiveness, obsession and jealousy, where there is no need or desire to control or dominate each other in order to feel more powerful.

True love happens when there are no conditions or expectations between each other but there is only unconditional giving and receiving.

True love happens when you have gone beyond the fear of losing and the fear of being alone.

True love happens when there is no dependence on each other for anything and there is no need left to use and manipulate each other for anything. What you do for each other is out of true love, not out of some selfish motive to gain something in return, not because of guilt or emotional blackmailing, not out of some need or dependence and definitely not out of ego.

True love happens when your ego or individual identity takes a back seat and there is mutual respect and gratitude for each other. True love happens when there is true understanding and acceptance between each other.

True love happens where there is oneness.

All this will happen naturally when both of them will leave their individual identity, their attachments, their fears, their expectations and become one energy and one consciousness, be it any relationship- brother sister, husband wife, parents children, guru disciple, etc.

Ask yourself this question. Have you ever experienced true love? I am sure there will be moments in your life when you had a glimpse of it. Understand the difference between love and attachment. Stop calling your egoic attachments and fears & insecurities as love when it is not true.

May god help you all experience true love!

27. Don't identify yourself with anything

Ego (I, me & myself) has this tendency to identify & attach itself with everything, for instance- with the body, with the thoughts, with the emotions, with desires, with family, with all material possessions, with name, powers, position, work, status, etc.

The more you identify yourself with all this, the more your ego or individual identity will become bigger and stronger. So in order to detach yourself with this ego and become one with your higher and true self, you have to understand and realize that nothing is yours. These thoughts are not yours, these emotions are not yours and these desires are not yours. Similarly these material possessions, powers, positions, status, business, family, etc is also not yours.

Always remember that all the thoughts, emotions, desires that come in your mind consciousness & awareness are not yours, so don't identify yourself with it. Everything is a form of energy and you are simply witnessing good and bad energy in your consciousness. For example rather than saying that "I am angry, I am sad, I am fearful", etc, learn to say that, "there is anger energy, fear energy, sad energy, etc, in my mind or in my consciousness". Then release and let go of what you no longer want in your presence or consciousness. You can do this through release sadhna. (To know more about release sadhna/meditation you can read my article on release sadhna/meditation)

Another example of this would be that rather than saying, "This is my house, my money, my jewelry, my parents, my husband or wife, my sister or brother, my children, my city, my country", etc, learn to say, "My infinite & pure consciousness is playing a temporary role, with complete detachment and unconditional love to play out the

(67)

responsibilities of this body. For non living objects you can say, "My infinite and pure consciousness is using them with complete detachment till the time this body needs it".

For that matter even your guru is not yours, you cannot possess him or her; you can only become one with him or her.

All the desires which come in your mind consciousness, presence, and awareness are not meant to be fulfilled. For example if you have a very deep desire to murder or to take revenge then you will not go ahead and fulfill this desire no matter how intense and deep it is. If you are conscious and aware then your consciousness will never let you do this. Your supreme and pure consciousness (Shiva) will give you the wisdom to do what is best for your being and for your ultimate good.

All kinds of thoughts, emotions and desires will come and go in your consciousness. You need to watch them and witness them, with this understanding that they are not yours and they do not belong to you. You can then choose or decide which thoughts, emotions or desires you need to retain & act upon and which to release and discard forever. Here I am not talking of any kind of suppression but just conscious dropping, releasing and letting go of this energy to attain freedom from it, which will only happen if you no longer identify yourself with it & able to look at it with complete detachment.

So once again always remember that, nothing is yours !

28. Complete surrender and complete faith is required to receive full grace of the guru.

All the sadhna/meditation is required till you purify yourself to the point where you can completely surrender yourself to your guru and have complete faith in him or her. Sadhna/meditation is needed till the day you become one with your guru, till the day you merge with his consciousness and energy. The day you reach this state of complete surrender and faith then no more sadhna/meditation is required. You just need to pray to your guru with complete faith and surrender and then everything starts happening on its own. Then guru's consciousness, knowledge, wisdom and energy flows through your mind, intellect, ego and make you do whatever is required or needed, whether it is sadhna/meditation or seva/selfless work or sankeertan/chanting or singing devotional songs (bhakti/devotion) or whether it is taking strong, bold steps and decisions or guiding somebody. You are no longer the doer, everything now happens through you by gurus and god's grace. Now all the effort happens not through your own will (will of mind and ego) but through your guru's will or divine/god's will. He will make you move, he will make you talk, he will make you rest.

Complete surrender and faith is when you don't use your own mind, intellect and ego anymore and just follow your guru's instructions, without any doubt, judgment or analysis.

When your guru tells you to do something and you no longer analyze or ask why, you just do it knowing in your heart and mind that your guru knows the best, then this is complete surrender and faith.

Complete faith is when you have no fear and no doubts even in the most difficult situations because you know that your guru is there to help you, guide you, take care of you whether he is in the physical dimension or subtle dimension, the only thing you need to do is to pray to your guru and ask for help, and follow the teachings of your guru completely.

29. True compassion

True compassion is the state beyond your mind, intellect, thoughts, emotions and logic. When you are overwhelmed by emotions, and feel the pain of the other inside you and get carried away by it and feel the sympathy towards that being, then this is not compassion.

Real compassion is having empathy not sympathy. It means you are not overwhelmed by other persons state but understand where he is at, understand his state and level of consciousness, understand his ignorance, understand his ego, have the wisdom to understand whether he truly wants help or not and is he ready to take help from you with faith and surrender or is it better to leave him in the hands of god and let god take care of the rest.

When you are overpowered by your emotions, you are an emotional being not a compassionate being. Similarly when you are overpowered by your intellect or logic, you are an intellectual or logical being, not a compassionate being. Real compassion is beyond all emotions and logic where divine presence operates in its full force and does what needs to be done through you, whether it is being firm, strong, harsh, and stern or being kind, loving, nurturing and caring. It will happen according to divine will and wisdom which is beyond all emotions and logic.

30. Go with your own pace and create your own destiny

If you truly want freedom or moksha in this life, you cannot move with the pace of the world, society or your family. You need to move with your own pace and let the world, society and family adjust to your pace and flow of things, which might take time but it will surely happen.

Don't feel bad or guilty about the fact that you are moving ahead of your family or society and leaving them behind because you have to understand that it is you who wants to get self realization or freedom/liberation in this life and not your family or society. The family and society may condemn you for it and will try to pull you back as they would not like you to move ahead of them. They will do it out of their ignorance, not knowing what they are truly doing, not realizing that they are trying to stop somebody from becoming a Buddha. But if you are sure of what you want, then you have to pursue your chosen path with the same intensity and pace, no matter what. Over a period of time if you remain strong and firm, then the whole world, society and your family will respect you and accept your path and let it be as it is. Even if that does not happen, it should not matter to you or affect you. You should remain at peace and have unconditional love for all.

Don't go with the flow and pace of your past sanchit karma and succumb to it but rather first get rid of your past sanchit karma & then create your own new flow of karma to create a new destiny for yourself. Going with the flow and accepting things the way they are, means you are letting your past karma and destiny to overpower you and rule you. So if you want to create a new destiny and be a master of it, you have to consciously not go with the flow of your past karma, mind patterns and conditionings and not accept them the way they are but rather make the attempt and effort with your guru's and god's grace to change them and break the flow of all the past sanchit karma ruling your life. If you are on the path of freedom/liberation/moksha then it is very important to do this, otherwise you will never be able to manifest what you want and you will never be free. (To know more about karma you can read the article on theory of karma)

31. Can you receive divine grace through a false guru?

The answer is yes. I can tell you from my personal experience that in order to receive divine blessings and grace you just need to be a true and deserving disciple. When I say true and deserving, it means you should have absolute faith and surrender towards your guru. You should be honest, transparent and pure from within. You should strictly follow your guru s teachings and apply it in your life and do regular sadhna/meditation taught to you by your guru without any expectations. You should constantly work towards your inner purification to remove all the fear, anger, jealousy, hatred, attachments, addictions, greed, ego, etc. If you are a true and deserving disciple you will receive divine grace through a false guru also, for that matter even through a dead stone or a tree, etc.

But if you are not a true and deserving disciple which means you don't have complete faith and surrender (you have doubts), you are not honest and transparent, you don't follow and apply your guru s teachings, you don't do your sadhna/meditation regularly and don't work towards your inner cleansing and purification, in that case you will not receive any divine grace and blessings even if there is god standing in front of you. So it is more important to make yourself deserving rather than worrying about the medium from where you will receive divine grace. If you truly deserve, you will receive it no matter what. Where, when and how you will receive it, that does not matter but if you do not deserve it, you will surely not receive it from anywhere.

Note : – But at the end let me make one thing very clear that what I have said above does not imply or mean that you allow anyone playing a role of a guru to take advantage of you physically, financially, mentally, emotionally, etc. It also does not imply or mean that you accept anyone as your guru. Only if you feel a connection and a pull initially and can completely relate with him or her then you accept that being as your guru and more importantly you should feel positive, peaceful in his or her presence irrespective of what he is doing externally.

32. Can one eat non vegetarian food on the spiritual path?

According to my guru Avdhoot Baba Shivananda, one can eat egg, fish and chicken but one should try to avoid eating red meat. He also says one should not eat snake, cow and pig meat at all.

Most importantly I feel that even eating plant and fruit is in a way non vegetarian because they are alive and have life or subtle life force energy in them, so killing them and eating is also against nature. In the olden times saints and rishi's used to wait under a tree for the fruit to fall on its own before they could eat it. It was considered wrong to even pluck the fruit from the tree against the wish of the tree. So if you wish to be a vegetarian, you need to be a complete vegetarian like in the olden times, otherwise don't call yourself a complete vegetarian.

Secondly according to my experience, when someone cooks vegetarian food with lot of anger, hatred, pain, etc then it makes the food non vegetarian because the energy of the food will have lot of anger, hatred, pain, etc in it. On the other hand when someone cooks even non vegetarian food with lot of love, gratitude, kindness and compassion, then it will turn that food into vegetarian food as it will have lot of energy of love, compassion, kindness and gratitude in it.

Thirdly before eating any food if you first offer it to your guru and god/deity, it will turn into positive energy because the guru's/gods/deity's positive energy will transmute all the negative energy of food into positive energy.

Finally I would add that while doing shakti/devi sadhna and hanuman sadhna, one should avoid non vegetarian food, alcohol and smoking completely for better and faster results.

33. Theory of karma

There are three forms of karma, one is prarabhdha karma which is already acted out whether in this life or past life, which means teer kamaan se nikal gaya hai (the arrow has left the bow). These karma's are already acted out by you so you will have to face the consequences of both good and bad prarabhdha karma, though the impact of it can reduce through your sadhna/ meditation and god's grace provided you learn your spiritual lessons but the fact is that you cannot escape prarabhdha karma completely. Then comes your sanchit karma which is still in the emotion and thought form, at thinking and emotional level, not still acted out, which means teer kamaan mein hai par abhi chala nahi hai (the arrow is still in the bow, has not left the bow yet). This sanchit karma can be changed or released as both good and bad thoughts and emotions can be changed or released. Then comes kriyaman karma which are all the psychic impression s stored in your subconscious and unconscious mind, which has not yet taken a form of a thought or emotion, which means abhi teer kamaan mein aaya hi nahi hai (the arrow is not yet formed /made so not in the bow yet). These psychic impressions stored in your subconscious and unconscious mind can also be changed or dissolved through your sadhna/meditation and by consciously releasing the psychic impressions from your subconscious mind.

These impressions (good and bad) stored in your subconscious when triggered or activated will eventually take a form of thought & emotion (good and bad) and thought & emotion will eventually turn into action (good and bad). Once acted out, you will have to face the consequences of it whether good or bad, either in this life or next life which then becomes your prarabhdha karma.

One more important thing to note is that no amount of good karma can cancel or dissolve the impact and consequences of bad karma. Both will have different consequences. For example if you do lot of humanitarian work, charity, etc, it does not mean it will cancel out the act of murder which you did consciously or unconsciously. You will still face consequences of both good and bad karma separately. The only way to get rid of your bad sanchit and kriyaman karma is by learning your spiritual lessons and through release and purification sadhna/ meditation and definitely through grace of god. And this grace you will receive only when you truly deserve it by doing your sadhna/meditation, seva/selfless work, good karma/good actions, and by having bhakti/devotion, faith, surrender and by following the teachings of your guru. Also unconditional love, forgiveness, gratitude meditation and release meditation will help to dissolve your (sanchit, kriyaman) karmic patterns and structure. As I said before, prarabhdha karma cannot be dissolved completely, you can only reduce its impact and time to whatever extent possible, so when prarabhdha karma is on the surface, it is the best time to learn your spiritual lessons and grow spiritually.

Also one more important thing to note here is that, for example you harm someone financially but due to this, that person and his family also goes through emotional, mental and physical pain, then you will also have to face the consequences of this karma not just financially but also mentally, emotionally and physically. Everyone will have to face the consequences of their good and bad karma eventually, it may not necessarily be the way you like it or want it.

One more clarity regarding this subject I want to give to all of you is that no one can give you healing or enlightenment or anything just like that. You get healed or enlightened or self realized because of your prarabhdha karma. If it is in your prarabhdha karma to receive, you will get it anywhere and through anyone but if it is not in your prarabhdha, you will not get it anywhere or through anyone. Positive and good prarabhdha karma can be created by undying faith and surrender towards your guru and god/deity, by doing sadhna/ meditation, seva/selfless work, good karma, bhakti/devotion and by applying the teachings of your guru in your life.

Everyone has to work out their karma on their own. Your past and present actions/karma will determine or create your future prarabhdha karma.

Whatever I received through my guru was in my prarabhdha karma. I would have received it anywhere, because I was meant to receive it. That is why guru s job is only to guide and help the disciple to get rid of bad or negative sanchit karma and bad or negative kriyaman karma of the past so that it does not take the shape of future prarabhdha karma and guru's job is also to help the disciple to do good or positive karma in the present so that it creates good or positive prarabhdha karma in the future. The rest will happen on its own

If what I have stated above is not true, then all the saints and gurus in the past or even in the present times could have healed everyone on this planet earth and dissolved the entire karmic structure of everyone. But they cannot do it because even they cannot go against the spiritual laws, karmic laws or laws of universe.

Why gurus or saints are able to help only few of them? Why not everyone? The only answer is, that it was according to their prarabhdha karma. Saints and gurus cannot be biased towards the only few who come to them. They are supposed to have such a big heart and so much compassion that if it is possible they would heal everyone and make everyone free from their karma, not just a few. They cannot do it because they are bounded and tied by the law of karma.

34. Are you truly growing and evolving spiritually?

I have seen many sadhaks/seekers relating their spiritual growth to the number of levels or courses they have done in their sadhna/meditation, for example to think, that if they have done five levels or courses, they are more spiritually evolved as compared to those who have just done two levels or courses.

It's amazing to see that so many of you get easily trapped in the web created by your ego and mind, which only indicates your lower level of consciousness and awareness. You will not come to know whether you are growing spiritually or not just by the number of levels or courses you have completed or by the number of sadhnas/meditations you have done or by the number of powers or siddhies you have gained or accumulated. You will know that you are growing spiritually when your inner peace and harmony is increasing, no matter what your outside situation or circumstances are. You will know when feeling of unconditional love, forgiveness and gratitude is increasing within you. You will know when your level of awareness and consciousness is increasing, which means you will be aware of your intentions, thoughts, feelings, emotions and actions all the time. You will know when your impurities of kam (sex/lust), krodh (anger), lobh (greed), moh (attachment) and ahankar (ego) are decreasing. You will know when your fear decreases and inner strength and courage increases. When your hatred, jealousy, desires reduce. When your need to take reduces and your ability to give increases. If all this is not happening, no matter how many levels you do or sadhnas/meditations you do or siddhies or powers you gain, I can assure you that you are then not growing or evolving spiritually at all.

So please stop fooling yourself and for once be honest to yourself and ask yourself, if you are truly growing or evolving spiritually. If yes, then how much as compared to your past? How much more you need to work on yourself? Be always aware and conscious of the mind, ego tricks and traps which will prevent you from truly growing and evolving.

Always remember: - The only purpose of all the sadhnas/meditations is to purify your inner self and take you to deeper levels of peace, harmony and bliss! Everything else is ego, mind trick and trap.

35. Qualities of a true spiritual leader or spiritual guide

1. A true leader or guide will be honest and transparent.

2. A true leader or guide will be selfless and working for the higher good of the people keeping in mind their best interests.

3. A leader or guide will have empathy and compassion. He or she will have the ability to understand the minds and egos of others and deal with it accordingly.

4. They will have the ability to look at the bigger picture with absolute clarity as they would be seeing things from a higher level. At ground level you can only see what is in front of you which is a very narrow vision. When you see things from higher level you have a broader view.

5. A true leader or guide will be fearless and will have the courage to face challenges with a positive outlook. They are not bothered about what people say but are more focused on giving 100% in whatever they do no matter how much opposition or criticism they face.

6. Their approach will be direct and straightforward. They will not be double faced and hypocrites. They will be the same inside and outside both. They will have only one face for themselves and for others, not two faces.

7. They will have humility and gratitude. They will have the quality to give and share, not keep everything to themselves.

8. Feeling of hatred, vengeance, greed will not be there in a true leader. He or she will not be running after fulfilling his or her selfish interests and egoic satisfaction.

9. A true leader or guide will be very experienced in his field. He will not guide others based on theoretical knowledge but will guide on basis of his experiences. They would have

learnt and grown in their path for many years. They will be able to talk with confidence & authority because of their very rich and profound experience.

10. They will have very good communication skills and clarity when they talk. They will talk with wisdom.

11. They will have the ability to inspire and motivate others

12. True leaders or guides are not fake so they don't try to be somebody they are not. They have their own unique individuality and persona.

13. True leaders or guides have always been good students or learners in the past giving due respect to their teachers and guides.

14. They are always hard working, determined, strong, dedicated and focused. They are always consistent and regular in their work and practices.

15. They will have the ability to act according to what they say. They will practice what they preach. They will have strong will power and the ability to manifest what they say through their actions, hard work, dedication, focus, commitment.

16. They will act consciously and have the ability to make people more aware and conscious of what they are doing. They will have the ability to go deeper within them and introspect or contemplate and help others to do the same. They will have strong intuitive powers.

17. True leaders or guides have the ability to help others learn and grow in their respective field of work or life in general with a very selfless attitude.

18. They will have the ability to make everything simple and easy for others. They will have the power and ability to resolve problems of people who come to them.

19. They have absolute and crystal clear clarity in what they do or say and therefore have the ability to give clarity to others and remove their doubts and confusions. If they don't have clarity at a given point of time, then they will make sure that they get clarity before they proceed further. They will never proceed further with any doubt and confusion.

20. They will never encourage negativity or weakness of any kind. They will never complain rather they will see hard times as opportunities to learn and grow. They will be naturally creative and have unique ideas and approach towards life. They will always be open to learning and growth. They will be extremely receptive and open towards everything. They will be flexible by nature and not rigid, and will give enough space and freedom to others so that they can work on themselves, grow and learn.

36. Is there only physical rape or is there mental, emotional and spiritual rape also?

Do you ever realize that we all go through not only physical rape but mental, emotional and spiritual rape also? If you are not even aware of it how will you protect yourself from being raped in all these different dimensions? Have you ever thought that how many times you also would have consciously or unconsciously or ignorantly raped others emotionally and mentally?

I know all of you are very well aware of the physical rape as it happens in a very gross dimension but other dimensions maybe very subtle for you to be even aware of. So let me try and make you aware of it.

When I use the word mental rape, it simply means trying to control and manipulate other's thoughts, opinions and belief systems against their wish or free will.

When I talk of emotional rape, it means when you try to control and manipulate other's feeling and emotions for your own use or benefit. For example when you do emotional blackmailing which is against the wish or free will of that person, you are manipulating that person for your own advantage.

And when I talk of spiritual rape, it means when you are forced to do something which is against your wish by creating fear in you in the name of god, religion/spirituality or astrology, etc.

My spiritual journey so far, has taught me one thing that when you do anything against anyone's free will or wish is considered wrong. So if you are now more aware of it and if you can stop doing this with others and also not allow others to do this with you, then it will lead to more harmony, balance and peace in your life and in the lives of other people around you. Though this might require lot of strength, courage and awareness, but believe me it's worth it.

There is nothing wrong in giving/stating your point of view or opinion or feelings but at the same time you should be very careful about the fact that the other person is also given the same freedom to accept or reject your point of view or opinion or feelings. Between two adults, there should not be any force or pressure from any side to make the other person agree or accept anything. If both sides are open and receptive towards each other's thoughts, feelings and opinions then it will lead to better understanding of each other and there will be greater possibilities of peaceful resolution and understanding to happen. Even if there is no mutual agreement on an issue, atleast they will understand each other's point of view and accept each other the way they are without trying to change each other against each others wishes and give each other enough space and freedom so that both can follow their own individual journey with their own views, perceptions, beliefs and understandings.

37. Everything and everyone around you is nothing but a reflection of yourself?

Is this really true? I have heard many people talking about it. I have seen it being mentioned in many spiritual books. But the real question is whether it has some truth in it or not? Well the answer is No and Yes both. I am saying this from my personal experience and especially after experiencing the state of shoonya (nothingness) and a state of pure, supreme consciousness, I know for certain that this is not true at the individual consciousness level but true to some extent at the higher and supreme consciousness level.

Only an absolutely clean mirror can reflect your true self and there are hardly any clean mirrors around you where your true reflection can be perceived. When I say a clean mirror, I mean a mind which is pure, clean and empty with no ripples of any thoughts and emotions. How many people around us are living in this state and even if they are, then for how many hours they remain in this state?

Muddied water with garbage cannot show a reflection of you, only crystal clean pure water can do that. Thus very few siddha's (realized beings) or gurus have such pure, clean mind and they are in a pure consciousness state. This is one reason that most of the times they are simply nothing but just reflections of your true nature and self. Their mind and ego does not exist in that moment so what you perceive is nothing but your own image (mind and ego) in them. But if you are truly in such a presence of a divine being, you may or may not be in a position to see that reflection of yourself because of your own impurities, ego and lack of surrender. You may consciously or unconsciously block it yourself from seeing it. You may even get totally blanked out and silent in that moment due to the impact of such a powerful presence.

People around us are so full of their own shit and garbage, that they definitely cannot be reflections of our selves but they can be reflections of their own garbage, impurities and other stuff they possess within them. In no way they can act as clean mirrors for us to see our reflection. They can simply act as triggers in some situations, to take out suppressed and hidden sanchit karma and garbage from our deep subconscious and unconscious mind and heart center. This can be a big opportunity for us to become aware of our garbage and weaknesses so that we can clear and release it from our heart and mind and purify our inner selves.

Till now I was talking of individual consciousness. Only in the higher state of universal/collective mind and higher consciousness you experience your oneness with everyone and everything and in this state everyone and everything becomes a part of you so in other words they all become your reflections. There is a higher state than this, where you feel that nothing exists including you. Here you only experience the existence of pure consciousness and pure energy, so in this state, there will not be any reflections of any kind be it good or bad. These are very different and higher spiritual states, so please don't get all mixed up, rather try to keep your concepts clear. If you have no clarity on the spiritual path, you cannot proceed further.

38. Astrology and Spirituality

The first part of astrology is the outermost layer, which is nonessential. There everything is circumstantial, uncertain, and unpredictable. The more we talk about external happenings, the more there is coincidence. The second part is the middle layer, the semi-essential layer. There is possibility of transformation here if the right choice is made. The third part is the core, the essence. It cannot be changed. When it is known, the only way is to cooperate with it.

The real thing is the third. It is the quintessence of everything. It belongs to the innermost and is absolutely predetermined. The more one moves toward one's center, the nearer one comes to the essential, the predetermined part. With inner phenomena things begin to appear scientific, as if based on a definite law. Here they become more and more decisive. Here, someone with awareness will make the correct choice, and the right way is to start moving towards your center. A person who is in the darkness of ignorance, will drift into his destiny, putting up with whatever comes his way. So there are three areas of life. In the area which is the essential core, everything is predetermined. In the area which is peripheral everything is uncertain. To know this is to know the everyday, unpredictable world. There is another area which is in the middle. By knowing this, a person can save himself from trying to do the impossible, and he can do what is possible. If a person lives in the peripheral and middle areas in such a way that he begins to move towards the center, he will become spiritual. But if he lives in such a way that he is never able to move towards the center, his life will remain non spiritual. This is how my guru Osho has explained it.

But I would like to go ahead and explain in more detail. When I am talking about astrology, I want you to have a picture of the whole science from many angles, so that you can enter it without any fear or hesitation. When I talk about astrology, I am not talking about the ordinary astrologer whom you consult for small matters or problems of day to day life. But the average man's curiosity regarding astrology is just to know whether his daughter will get married or not, to know about career or financial situation or health or children, etc.

The core, the essence, cannot be changed. It is the part which is most difficult to understand. The second part is the middle layer, in which one can make whatever changes one wants. It is the semi-essential portion, in which you can make changes if you know how to, but without knowing how, no changes are possible at all. The third part is the outermost layer which is nonessential, about which we are all very curious to know and we go to consult astrologers only for the nonessential things.

I have been recently reading astrological charts and I totally agree with Osho that astrological and birth charts show and reveal karmic debts of the past and it also reveals the lessons that one needs to learn in this life, which is very important for one to progress and grow spiritually and eventually transform themselves, which Osho describes as the very essential and unconscious part. It also tells future possibilities of growth, learning, transformations and other opportunities. And shows areas where one may face difficulties for the higher purpose of growth and learning. This is the core and it gives a larger and bigger picture. And believe me it is very easy to know this bigger picture from your astrological birth chart or lagna chart which includes your karmic debts, your lessons and future possibilities of transformation.

Then, there is the subconscious and semi essential part which tells you where you have free will and where you dont have it. The areas where you have past karma and where you need to learn your lessons, you may not have complete free will and the areas where you don't have any major karma of the past and not any big lessons to learn, you may have complete free will and choice.

Then, there is this non essential area, your conscious part, the smaller aspects of your life which are linked with the unconscious and larger part - the core. If you change the very core, the smaller aspects (non essential area/conscious part) will change themselves. So in short, astrological chart reading should be done to know your core, your unconscious, which is your past life karmic debt and lessons to learn in this life, for spiritual growth and transformation. But if you don't bring any change and transformation in the larger unconscious part which is the core, then there will not be any change in the smaller areas which are non essential/conscious part and semi essential/sub conscious part.

I have been to many renowned astrologers in my life but unfortunately I have not seen astrologers reading the very essential part, which is the bigger and higher picture of learning and growth, which is the most important part. Rather I have seen them focusing on small things or making predictions about these smaller areas of life which is usually wrong, atleast in my case it has been proved wrong many times.

The problem is that nobody wants to work out their karma and learn their lessons, rather they all want some easy solutions to their problems and hurdles. That is why they all go to astrologers, not to find out about their karmic debt or to find out about which lessons they need to learn but rather they are also more interested in knowing about small non essential things of their life.

But the truth is that everyone eventually must work out their karma through hard work, sadhna or meditation, realizations and learnings, awareness, selfless service /seva, selfless love, compassion, empathy and by learning their lessons like forgiveness, love, kindness, hard work, detachment, etc in different areas of their lives.

No one can escape learning and growth and transformation because that is the essential, the core of our soul nature and being. If you do not work out your karma and learn your lessons in this life, then it will be carried forward in your larger unconscious mind, to your next lives which will then again affect your subconscious and conscious or smaller areas of your next life.

39. What are the spiritual lessons that all these 12 planets want you to learn through their placement in your astrological chart/lagna chart?

The placement of all these 12 planets in your birth chart or astrological chart/lagna or birth chart is for you to learn your spiritual lessons in this life. If you really learn your lessons then these planets give you beneficial and positive results. The planets are placed in 12 houses. There can be more than one planet in one house.

House 1: This is house of outer self (personality, body, appearance, self image and identity) and beginning years of your life.

House 2: This is house of money and material possessions earned by you.

House 3: This is house of early/lower education, communication, short trips, siblings, reading and writing.

House 4: This is house of parents, home and family.

House 5: This is house of children, love affairs, creativity and personal interests.

House 6: This is house of daily routine work (both at home and outside), diet and health.

House 7: This is house of marriage and long term business partnerships.

House 8: This is house of loss, detachment, death, sex, transformation, healing, inheritance, other people's money and resources, transcendence or going beyond.

House 9: This is house of higher education and spiritual growth.

House 10: This is house of career and reputation/status.

House 11: This is house of friends, social groups, associations and wishes, desires, goals.

House 12: This is house of subconscious and unconscious, hidden aspect of yourself and past life.

Following are the spiritual lessons that these planets are meant to teach you in the house and area it resides:-

Planet Sun gives you energy, success and leadership provided you learn the lesson of keeping your ego, dictatorship and authority aside. More importantly learn to let go of your ego.

Planet Moon gives you security provided you learn the lesson of controlling your reactions and emotions. Here I don't mean suppressing your emotions or reactions. I mean letting go and releasing your unnecessary emotions and reactions specially the negative ones. This will lead to emotional stability and peace within you. If you don't learn these lessons there will be lot of fluctuations and changing conditions in the area or house this planet resides.

Planet Mercury gives you ability to think, analyze and communicate, read and write provided you don't misuse any of it. When I say misuse I mean not harm anyone through your speech or writing and not judge or criticize anyone through your thinking or analysis. If you don't learn these lessons there will be lot of hurdles in your communication, thinking, reading and writing.

Planet Venus gives you love, pleasure and comforts provided you don't get too attached or obsessed with it.

Planet Mars gives you lot of courage, strength and intense energy to act provided you learn the lesson of letting go of your anger/aggression. Don't be over assertive or aggressive otherwise it may lead to conflict and fights. If you don't learn these lessons, there will be lot of fights and conflicts in the area or house it resides.

Planet Jupiter gives you lot of growth, higher knowledge and learning, joy and happiness, provided you learn to respect and surrender towards your guru/ teachers. Then you receive lot of divine grace.

Planet Saturn gives you slow but long lasting results, provided you learn the lessons of hard work, patience, responsibility, discipline, selflessness, practicality. If you don't learn these lessons, there will be lot of delays and hurdles, limitations and restrictions and frustration in the area or house this planet resides.

Planet Uranus gives you uniqueness, originality, freedom, independence, innovative ideas, intuitive awakening, replaces old with new, provided you evolve and grow, learn and change for the better. Also to learn the lesson of respecting your uniqueness, freedom and independence and at the same time respecting other people's uniqueness, independence and freedom also, which means not letting other people do anything against your free will, nor you do anything against other people's free will. If you don't learn these lessons, there will be lot of sudden shocks, disruptions and changes in the area or house this planet resides.

Planet Neptune gives you imagination and visualization provided you have realistic expectations, and learn the lessons of being practical and realistic and not have unrealistic expectations. If you don't learn these lessons, there will be lot of disappointment and confusion in the area or house this planet resides.

Planet Pluto gives you power, transformation, healing and detachment/transcendence, provided you go through some form of terrible suffering in your life and deal with it positively rather than negatively.

Planet Rahu gives you power and wealth, provided you learn the lesson of not misusing your power or wealth. If you don't learn these lessons, there will be lot of confusion, depression, emotional imbalance in the area or house this planet resides.

Planet Ketu gives you spiritual achievements and unexpected gains, provided you learn to let go of your ego and selfishness and become ego-less and selfless. If you don't learn these lessons, there will be lot of worry, anxiety, poor concentration and depression in the area or house this planet resides.

Placement of all these 12 different planets in 12 different houses in everyone's chart indicates which lesson they need to learn in which house or area of their life. Everyone must learn all their lessons in order to get material or spiritual success in this life.

40. Can you surrender totally without first being conscious totally?

It is very easy to say that I have surrendered myself but actually very difficult to do. The simple reason being that you cannot surrender something which you yourself are not totally conscious or aware of. Yes, it is definitely possible to surrender that part of you which you are conscious of, but how you can surrender that part which you yourself are not conscious or aware of.

There is a great possibility that your conscious mind/being may surrender, but your subconscious and unconscious mind/being may be holding itself back, not ready to surrender. For example, how can you surrender your ego when you yourself are not conscious and aware of its gross and subtle aspects? You can definitely surrender that part of your ego which you are conscious of but that part of ego which is still residing in your deep subconscious and unconscious, which is still not completely activated, cannot be surrendered. That is why it is always possible for any student or disciple to take a u turn during their journey, if they are overpowered by their subconscious and unconscious reactions, impressions and ego.

Even at the conscious level most of you only surrender selectively not totally. Total surrender of yourself means surrendering your identity, your attachments, your desires, your good and bad qualities, your good and bad karma. It is basically everything but in reality what do you do? You only surrender the bad part not the good part. Is this true and total surrender?

Contemplate on what I have said. You might understand the depth of what I am talking about here.

That is why on the spiritual path it is very important to raise your level of consciousness through acquiring right knowledge and by doing sadhna or meditation. Once you are totally conscious and aware, you can release, let go and surrender.

41. Are you completely free to live your life the way you want to all the time? If not, then why? Here is the simple explanation for it.

We all deep down want to live our lives the way we want to but how many of us truly live like that?

We are all caught up in this game of life and we have to play this game well in order to accomplish what we want through this game. Can you all the time play this game the way you want to? Think about it. If not then why? What is stopping you? What is holding you back?

Well if you think deeply, you will understand and realize that there are three things that will not let you be yourself or let you play this game of life the way you want to. These three things are your fears, your attachments and your desires. To start with, in the first place, it is your desires and attachments due to which you are in this game. It is your own desires and attachments which compel you to play this game of life again and again. With no desires and attachments you will have this freedom to decide whether to play this game of life or not. But right now with so many attachments and desires you have no choice but to play this game and on top of it there is also this pressure of playing it well.

Because of your fears, attachments and desires you have to please everyone's egos, you have to adjust and make compromises. In order to fulfill your desires you have to make sure that your boss and customers are happy at your workplace, and at home you have to make sure that your parents, wife, husband, etc, are happy, as you are dependent on them. In order to fulfill your desires you will always be dependent on others, so it is but obvious that you cannot do everything the way you want to but rather do the way others want it. In this way you can make others happy and when they are happy, in return they can fulfill your needs and desires. The more the desires/needs, the weaker the person would be because he or she is now more dependent on others and hence there is more chance or possibility of him or her being exploited and manipulated by others.

The more attached the person is towards other people, things/material possessions, self-identity, self-image, the more fearful he or she will be, because he or she will always have this fear of losing those people, things/material possessions, self-image and self-identity. The more fearful the person is, the weaker he or she will be. And as you know weak people are easily manipulated and exploited by the stronger ones. And it's also a fact that not everyone is weak or strong all the time. The same person who is weak in one situation can be strong in some other situation depending on his desires, attachments and fears in the given situation.

But people who are truly desireless, fearless and detached with absolutely no desires, fears or attachments, are very strong within, whether they show their strength or not. They can surely never be manipulated and exploited by others. Even though they have strength and power, they will not exploit or manipulate the weaker lot because they will have no desire to do so. These people will have the freedom to choose whether to play this game of life or not and if they chose to play then they will be able to play the way they want to, but the irony is that because of no desires left they will not wish to play this game of life at all. They will only be in this game to work out all their remaining karma or become the medium of the divine and simply let god play its game through them.

42. Do you stop enjoying life once you reach a state of total vairagya or desirelessness?

The answer is no. Once you go beyond all your desires and reach a state of vairagya, you still continue to enjoy life completely and fully. What it simply means, is that you are no longer addicted to any person or anything anymore. Desire, after a period of time becomes an addiction which further takes a form of greed if not controlled. What usually happens when you don't get the person or thing that you desire or are addicted to? You start missing that thing and you go through immense pain and misery. But when you have no desire, you have no addiction and hence there is no reason for you to go through any pain or misery. So you enjoy life totally and completely with no addiction, pain or misery.

People with no desires will enjoy with whatever they have, in a given moment and will always be grateful for it, because they never wanted anything in the first place, but still they are getting it. For example if they are given good clothes to wear or good house to live in, then they will enjoy that and be grateful for that but at the same time they will not miss it or feel bad if it is taken away from them because deep down they never had any desire for it, so it will not make any difference to them. Another example would be, if they are given good food to eat, they will enjoy it but if it is not given to them they will not miss it or feel bad about it, because they don't have desire or addiction for it.

A person with no desires and expectations will have much more fulfilling, happier and peaceful relationships with people around him or her as compared to a person who has desires and expectations. And that is because in all forms of relationship, a desireless person will be able to give everything selflessly and unconditionally without expecting anything in return. At the same time he or she will enjoy their relationships to the fullest. People who are desireless will live in the present moment completely, totally and fully and then move on to the next moment with total acceptance and gratitude.

43. Happiness that comes from within is permanent. So first learn to be happy in your own being.

Happiness that you seek outside of yourself is temporary and will not last forever but happiness which comes from within is permanent and will last forever. Happiness that you seek outside through material possessions, ambitions, relationships, family, etc is temporary in nature because this happiness is dependent on outside things, situation and people. And as you know you can never control situations or people the way you want to. There will always be ups and downs. The more you will be dependent on others for your happiness, the more you will be exploited and manipulated by them. The more you will depend on material possessions for your happiness, the greedier you will become. The desire to get more and more will never let you be happy and contented.

That is why I say that you first learn to be happy in your own inner being then you will not have to depend on outside things, situations and people for happiness. Remember those moments when you were a child or a kid. Were you then not happy in your own being? Was then your happiness controlled by outside things and people? Were you then, not just happy being yourself, not bothered by anything around you, living in the present moment, enjoying every moment? Can't you awaken that child within you again? Well of course you can if you truly want to. Start with doing all the things that you used to do as a kid. This will begin to give you happiness and this happiness will come from inside you not outside you. The next thing you can do is to be always grateful for all that you have, rather than complaining about what you don't have. If you can always fill your heart with the feeling of gratitude, then believe me you will always be happy. Finally if you start accepting and giving people unconditional love with no expectations in return, you can always remain happy. If you learn to be happy from within, you will no longer have to depend on outside world and people for your happiness. This happiness will be there with you all the time and will never go away. So from now on stop being a beggar and become a king. Share this happiness of your being with others and live like a king from within. Then there will be no need to beg or expect from others to do things for you to make you happy. This will make you feel freer and lighter in your being. People, who can be happy inspite of being alone, are people who will depend less on others for happiness and vice versa.

44. How to remain positive all the time and how does this positive attitude help in our spiritual path?

It is very important to have a positive attitude on the spiritual path otherwise spiritual growth is not possible. Positive attitude helps us to deal with negative situations and people in a positive way which helps us to work out our negative karma very quickly. Positive attitude gives us positive strength and energy to face everything in life and not run away from it. It also gives us the strength and courage to take responsibility for our actions and karma, and work on ourselves & our karma, rather than blaming or criticizing others for it. On the spiritual path we can only work on our inner selves and bring that change and improvement that we are seeking for ourselves. Once we change and improve then others will also change. Even if others don't change, at least we will grow spiritually. Positive attitude helps us to see the positive side of things and helps us to see the growth and learning opportunities in adverse, difficult and negative situations.

In order to maintain this positive energy within us all the time, we should first free ourselves from all negative energy within us by doing release sadhna/meditation. To know more about release process you can read the article on release sadhna/meditation. Secondly we should learn to forgive and let go. Thirdly we should always be grateful for what we have rather than complaining about what we don't have. And fourthly we should always accept and love people unconditionally without any expectations. If we fill our inner being with the energy of gratitude and unconditional love all the time, we will always remain happy and positive. Finally we have to always remember one most important thing on this spiritual path that whatever is happening is happening for our ultimate good. Whatever is happening is happening for our spiritual growth and learning. We might not be able to see the bigger picture behind what is happening (whether good or bad), but one day we will be able to see and understand it. Till then we have to deal with everything positively and with lot of patience.

45. Forgiveness, Gratitude and Unconditional Love sadhna/meditation

Apart from release sadhna/meditation, forgiveness, gratitude & unconditional love sadhna/meditation is also very important for inner purification and faster spiritual growth. I am saying this from my personal experience. You will be able to see the difference yourself once you start practicing these sadhnas/meditations every day. The process of forgiveness, gratitude & unconditional love sadhna/mediation is very simple and easy. I have already discussed with you a shorter version of it in my earlier articles, but here I will give you a more detailed version of it.

You start this sadhna/meditation by first invoking your guru and god (whichever god you believe in whether in form or formless dimension). Then you pray to your guru and god to bless you and guide you in your sadhna/meditation. The next step is to think about all those people who have harmed you or hurt you in any way, at any point of time in your life. You then mentally forgive them for what they have done realizing and understanding that whatever they did or are doing is because of their ignorance and lower state of consciousness. They don't have that level of consciousness to understand what they are really doing. They are doing it because they are overpowered by the impact of their own sanchit karma or psychic impressions stored in their subconscious and unconscious mind. So as you forgive them, you consciously let go of all the pain, anger and negativity you have for them in your heart and mind, realizing and understanding that this anger and negativity will only harm you in the long run. Then you consciously and mentally ask for forgiveness from all those whom you have harmed or hurt in any way consciously or unconsciously so that they can free themselves from all the pain, anger and negativity that they have for you in their heart and mind. Once this is done you fill your heart and entire being with the feeling and energy of gratitude. You thank god for this breath because of which you are alive and living every day. Thank god for all parts of your body functioning properly. Thank your body also for day and night working for you. Be grateful for it. Thank god for your well functioning mind and intellect. Be grateful for it. Thank your mind for obeying your commands and thank your intellect for giving you the ability to analyze and understand. Thank god for giving you the strength and energy to work hard in your job, business and home. Be grateful for what you have earned and received till now in your business or job and also for what you have received from your family and friends. At this point of time only focus on what you have got not what you have given and be grateful for that. Thank god for this creation of planet earth and the whole universe. Mentally thank the planet earth for all that it has given to you, for example, all the natural resources, etc and be grateful for that. Be grateful for whatever has happened in your life till now and for everything that will happen in future, because you know and understand that everything that has happened and will happen is only for your spiritual growth and learning, so thank god for all your growth and learning. After doing this you fill your heart and your entire being with the feeling and energy of unconditional love. You feel, imagine and visualize that this love energy is continuously flowing from your heart and both your hands . You feel the love towards your body and send this love energy from your heart to every part of your body. You feel the love for your family, friends and colleagues and send this love energy to all of them. Also send this love energy to your workplace and home. Then feel this love for everyone that you have known in your life and send this love energy to all of them including people who have not been good to you. Then feel love for mother earth and the whole universe, and send this love energy to the planet earth and the whole universe. Then, send this love energy to all the events of the past and future. Finally end this sadhna/meditation by feeling gratitude and love towards your guru and god.

46. When you are in the present moment or in a state of no mind you come closer to experiencing god or supreme consciousness/supreme energy

The whole purpose of doing any sadhna or meditation is to purify your inner being and to empty the mind so that you reach a state of no mind and experience silence and stillness. You can only experience your soul (higher consciousness) and god (supreme consciousness) in deep silence and stillness when you go beyond the mind.

If you release all the psychic impressions and memories of the past and release all the worries, fears and desires of the future, you will be able to live in the present moment giving your 100% in that moment and accepting every moment as it comes and being grateful for that. If there are no thoughts of past and future, then living in the present moment helps you to go beyond the thinking mind and makes you come closer to god consciousness and energy. So let go of your past and surrender your future in the hands of your guru or god, and you start living in the present moment to experience your soul, god consciousness and energy, giving your 100% in whatever you are doing in that present moment.

It is important to make a note of one thing that if you cannot release or let go of your desires, then fulfill your desires but do not suppress them as any kind of suppression causes more harm. Unwanted and negative desires or habits have to be either released or reprogrammed through neuro linguistic programming of the mind patters or neural networks. To change any negative pattern, habit or desire through this process, you need to stop doing what you wish to change for minimum of 21 days and instead do what you would ideally like to do in that place. You have to do this for 21 days without giving a break for even one day. You can pray to your guru and god to give you the required strength and will power to do it. It is scientifically proven that it takes minimum 21 days for any mind pattern to transform or change.

47. Don't run after spiritual experiences. They will come and go.

You will have different forms of spiritual experiences during different stages of your spiritual journey. But its important for you to know that these experiences will come and go, and you will not be able to control them. So you should not expect or desire any experience rather you should just let experience happen naturally, when they are meant to happen. You should only focus on doing what you need to do on your spiritual path which is to acquire right spiritual knowledge because right spiritual knowledge gives you clarity and awareness and raises your level of consciousness. This is called gyan yoga. At the same time, you should have complete surrender, faith, bhakti/devotion towards your guru or deity/ishta/god. This will help to purify and soften your heart which is very important on the spiritual path. This is called bhakti yoga. Then along with it, you also do good karma, sadhna/meditation and selfless work or niswarth seva in your day to day living. Witnessing is also very important which you should do within yourself all the time. You should witness or watch your intentions, thoughts, feelings, emotions and actions all the time. This will help you to become more aware and conscious. This is called karma yoga.

It is also important for you to realize and understand that everyone has its own unique spiritual journey, so you should not compare your spiritual experiences with other people's spiritual experiences. Comparing is an act of ego, so you should avoid doing it. I have seen lot of times people hallucinating and imagining spiritual experiences especially when they are not having any real spiritual experiences. It is very easy to be fooled by your own mind, because it is very powerful and it can create all kinds of experiences for you, if you intensely desire it. So be very careful and not get trapped by your mind. The spiritual journey is actually meant to go beyond mind and all mind experiences. So my advice to all of you is to not run after these mind experiences, but rather empty your mind and reach a state of no mind, where you experience the real stuff which is peace, silence, stillness and eventually nothingness and pure consciousness.

48. Low, negative and difficult phase of your life is more important for real spiritual growth and learning as compared to high and positive phase of your life.

If you are a true and honest seeker and if you truly and honestly want spiritual growth, then you will not complain, feel bad or low, when you come across negative or difficult times of your life, rather you will see it as an opportunity for your spiritual growth and learning and make the best of it. During tough and negative times all your negative sanchit karma will come up on the surface in the form of thoughts, feelings, emotions and desires. You can use this time as an opportunity to work out your negative sanchit karma and release all your negative thoughts, feelings, emotions and desires or habits through release sadhna/meditation. (To know more about release meditation you can read my article on release sadhna/meditation). This will also be a good time to learn your spiritual lessons that you are supposed to learn in this life. You need to contemplate and introspect within yourself to know which spiritual lessons you need to learn in this negative and difficult situation. For example, the lesson can be of forgiveness or detachment, etc. In the spiritual path, difficult and tough times are also very important to thrash and break the ego to eventually make the ego surrender.

As a spiritual seeker you should be always prepared and ready to face difficult/tough times and negative prarbhdha karma with a positive attitude and always see it as an opportunity for your spiritual growth and learning. (To know more about karma read article on theory of karma)

49. Who is your soulmate?

In today's world lot of people are searching for their soulmate not realizing that it is not what it seems or looks like. This is because most of the people don't even know what soulmate means. Soulmate means your connection with someone at the soul level. It does not necessarily mean that it has to be your husband-wife, partner or lover but it can be anyone with whom you have soul connection, be it your guru, brother or sister, children, friend, colleague, etc.

The most important thing to understand or realize here is that for you to have any connection at the soul level, you first need to or rather have to evolve at the soul level yourself. That will only happen through spiritual progress, when you either experience your soul or become one with your soul. So the fact is that if you have not yet become one with your soul or experienced your soul or made connection with your soul, then how can you even think of becoming one with someone else's soul or making connection with someone else's soul.

Another important thing to understand here is that the day you realize or experience your soul and become one with your soul, you will be able to connect with everyone's soul. Hence from thereon everyone will become your soulmate. Because at the higher spiritual dimension there are no separate souls that exist rather there is only one and same soul for everyone which is called supreme soul or param atma, and we all have this same soul or are connected with this same soul or in other words we are this supreme soul or param atma. It is only matter of realizing it or experiencing it. So rather than waiting for your soulmate you work towards becoming one with your soul so that everyone can become your soulmate.

In this worldly dimension when you are attracted to someone or feel good or bad towards someone, it is mainly due to your karmic connection of past life or this life with that person or to settle your karmic account of credit and debit or karmic account of give and take with that person. The moment this karmic account is settled you will neither feel good or bad towards that person nor will you feel any attraction towards that person rather you will feel nothing or neutral towards that person. So if you get attracted to someone, don't mistake him or her as your soulmate, because as you now know that this is not the truth.

50. You are the master, and your mind and ego is your servant.

When I say that you are the master, and your mind and ego is your servant, I mean that your real or true self or your soul is the master and your mind and ego is the servant. Don't ever let your mind or ego become the master, because if that happens, your ego and mind (karma) will overpower you and control you and will make you act or work according to its wishes whether it is good or bad, right or wrong. If you succumb in front of your mind, ego or negative karma, you will not be able to grow spiritually, and you will also not be able to bring about the changes you are seeking in your life.

So the only way not to succumb in front of your ego or mind or karma is when you awaken your will power (icha shakti), soul power (atma shakti) and knowledge power that comes from your soul (gyan shakti jo atma se aati hai) through your sadhna/meditation, inner purification, guru and gods grace and by raising your level of consciousness and awareness. With the help of this strong will power (icha shakti), soul power (atma shakti) and knowledge power (gyan shakti) you will be able to witness, watch, direct and control your mind and ego. In other words, you will be able to harness and direct your karma, ego and minds energy in the right and positive direction. This will give you inner strength and courage to face and deal with your mind, ego and karma in a positive way. This will help you to overcome your weaknesses, dissolve your bad karma and eventually help you to go beyond your mind, ego and experience the ultimate truth.

Part B: My spiritual experiences, realizations and learnings

Chapter One: Spiritual experiences in my childhood

1. Shirdi Sai Baba, my first guru who touched & transformed the deepest core of my heart.

This was the time when my mom (foster mother) who was a devotee of Shirdi Sai Baba (who is no longer in the physical body), took me to Shirdi and for the first time I experienced something very divine. I must have been 7 or 8 years old. I am deeply grateful to my mother for introducing me and leading me to divine presence of Shirdi Sai Baba. I don't remember my exact age but it was during this time that I also saw a movie called Shirdi Ke Sai Baba which had Manoj Kumar & Hema Malini as actors in it, but the actor who was playing the role of Sai Baba in that movie was the one who touched my heart the most. After watching this movie, I cried for many days, as it must have opened and purified my heart (anahat charka). Since then, I became a sincere devotee of Sai Baba and my path of bhakti yoga started without my knowing it. From then on I used to often talk to Sai Baba in the subtle dimension, share all my problems and fears with him, seek his guidance and love and pray to him almost all the time for everything. I experienced lot of miracles in his presence which I know most of the Sai devotees have experienced in their lives.

When I was around 8 to 10 years old, I had been watching lot of horror movies, because of which I could not sleep alone in the night in my bedroom. Every time I closed my eyes I used to see lot of horrifying faces and felt extreme fear inside me. I had been a great devotee of Shirdi Sai Baba since I was a kid, so I used to pray and talk to him every night. So I prayed to him again with all my intense devotion towards him to help me release this fear and help me sleep. Meanwhile, I also played some Shirdi Sai Baba bhajans(devotional songs) which I loved listening to every night. After some time, I felt Sai Baba's subtle presence next to me putting his hand on my head and I suddenly felt all my fear being washed away with his grace. I felt very peaceful, relaxed and sleepy. I had a wonderful sleep that night. After this experience, I realized the power and importance of prayer in my life especially when done with great devotion, love and faith.

After sometime I used this power of prayer again, when I was in severe physical pain and no medicine was able to give me any relief. So I prayed again with lot of intensity and faith to Shirdi Sai Baba. While I was praying I suddenly saw his face in front of me and guess what? My pain was completely gone as if it was never there. Bhakti yoga deepens our faith & surrender and opens & purifies our heart which is very important in our spiritual path and this phase of my life did the same for me. This was a higher divine purpose of Sai Baba coming to my life at such an early age.

2. The influence of Jesus Christ in my school days

I studied in a convent school so we were all the time surrounded by nuns and did our morning prayers everyday to Jesus Christ. It created a deep impact on my psyche in my growing years and one such incident I would like to share here. There was a church in my school. I used to go to that church before every test or exam. Every time I scored good marks I would go and thank Jesus Christ, but whenever I scored badly I would go and complain to him. So one of these days when I was complaining to him, I intuitively felt that he was trying to tell me, that it was very selfish of me that I come and spend time in the church only when there is a test or exam, not otherwise. I immediately realized my mistake and from there on every Saturday I would go to this church, drink the holy water which was kept there and would sit in silence for a few minutes and offer my prayers if I had to. I found the energies of the church to be very peaceful and that is one reason I was attracted to this place.

3. Chanting of gayatri mantra during my school years

During my school years someone told me the importance of gayatri mantra saying that gayatri devi was the devi/goddess of gyan or knowledge and chanting this mantra will help to improve my concentration and help me in my studies. So I started mentally chanting this mantra and after sometime I experienced some bright light at my third eye. These glimpses of light would come and go but I could not understand the relevance of it at that time, as I was not so spiritually mature that time. But it did help my mind to become more stable and definitely improved my concentration.

4. How my dog made me realize the importance of unconditional love and detachment

My dad got a small Pomeranian dog for me when I was 13 years old and because of him I experienced what a mother would experience when she has a child. When he came, he was just a month old and for the first three nights I could not sleep as I had to make sure that he slept well, because he was just separated from his mother. I had to give all my love, care and warmth to this puppy, which I did. I later named him Fedo. I did everything for him, from giving bath to cleaning his vomit to feeding him, etc. With time I got deeply attached to him and always felt unconditional love flowing from my heart towards him, no matter what. I received the same unconditional love from him even at times when I was angry or sad. This definitely opened & purified my heart (heart or anaahat charka) even more. This was a phase in my life where I understood that true divine love was all about giving without conditions or expectations. The only problem was my attachment to him which was so deep that it caused lot of pain to me especially when I saw him being hurt or in pain or when he was left alone in the house. It was unbearable at times. Even when something very minor would happen to him, it was very traumatic and painful for me. This went on for many years and then I realized that I can't take this pain anymore and I have to learn to detach myself from him if I really want freedom from this pain. As time passed, I also realized that this life itself (with all its good & especially bad circumstances & events) is the guru or the teacher & we have to keep learning the lessons, that it is trying to teach us for our own spiritual growth

Chapter Two: Spiritual experiences in my teens and adulthood

1. The turning point in my life's journey after reading the book "Autobiography Of A Yogi"

This was the time when I was around 17 or 18 years old and through someone I came to know about pranic healing classes, so I immediately got myself registered for the class. This was the first time that I understood the impact of pranic energy or life force energy in my life. While I was learning, practicing and taking higher level classes of pranic healing, I bought a book on pranic healing in which I saw a picture of Maha Avatar Babaji and I got mesmerized looking into his eyes and felt deep connection with him. I then inquired about him from my pranic healing teacher and he gave a small intro about kriya yog and babaji, and then gifted me this book called Autobiography of a Yogi.

Before I further mention about this experience, I would like to tell you about a deep spiritual experience that I had when I was 7 years old. I was once lying down with my eyes closed. I felt some throbbing sensation at my third eye (the point between the two eyebrows) & then saw some flashes of light. My attention was drawn towards it & I felt as if my consciousness is traveling through a very deep, dark hollow tunnel. Then I heard the voices of some saints or masters giving me the knowledge and experience of shoonya/nothigness. It went on for quite some time & when I got up after this experience, I did not understand anything as I was just 7 years old then & as time went by, I forgot about this experience completely.

When later in my life, I was reading this book "Autobiography Of A Yogi " during the year 1995-1996, I felt a sudden shift in my consciousness & I could easily understand every word written in that book. I was then able to understand the experience I had when I was 7 years old. I felt a strong urge & desire to leave everything & take sanyas (recluse). But I soon realized there is no need to escape or run away from life but rather have to be in it to attain my spiritual goals. This changed everything in my life, including my perceptions and I started inquiring about life and death and how to attain liberation from both. From here on my inner freedom became most important aspect in my life. I got myself enrolled in self-realization fellowship program of kriya yoga through correspondence and started receiving lessons on exercises, kriyas & meditation which I started practicing every day.

2. Arahatic Kundilini meditation course

When I was in my early 20's, I had attended a two day course on Arahatic Kundalini meditation which was taught by a tibetan monk. It was a long meditation of 2 hours which we were supposed to practice every day. After practicing for a few days a lot of good and bad experiences started happening and I did not know whom to contact and ask why & what was happening, as I was totally confused with what I was experiencing. So eventually I stopped practicing it but at the same time I also realized that it is important to have a personal guru who can guide you, support you and give you clarity, when you are stuck and confused especially at the beginning of your journey.

3. My deep realizations after reading books of Osho

During my days of graduation I used to have lot of free time and used to read lots of books on discourses of Osho. These readings purified my intellect and made it very sharp. And I soon realized that if your intellect is pure then you will be able to use your intellect to reject the knowledge which creates confusion and accept the knowledge which gives you more clarity and wisdom.

Osho' s teachings also gave me the courage to be myself no matter what the society says or thinks. His teachings made me fearless. It also helped me to understand the meaning of true relationship & true love. From there on I started experiencing all the relationships (with family & friends) on a very high level of consciousness with no expectations & no conditions & no bindings of any kind. It meant absolute freedom & true unconditional love with no attachments.

During this time I also practiced lot of meditations taught by Osho like dancing meditation, witnessing meditation, tratak/ candle light meditation and dynamic breathing meditation which made me feel very good from inside.

4. The experience of other healing and meditative practices on my spiritual path

During the years of my graduation 1996-1999, masters in business administration 2001-2003 and during my job as a training manager 2003-2005, I also got myself initiated into reiki healing, reiki mastership, crystal healing, angel healing, past life regression therapy, neuro linguistic programming course. The higher divine purpose was to learn these practices and have some very minor but very deep experiences which were essential to strengthen my faith. For example, while being initiated in reiki level 2, I had an experience which shook me from within. While I was being initiated, I felt and saw lot of spiritual masters around me and saw Shirdi Sai Baba taking my feet in his hands and dipping in a pot of water. Seeing this I could not hold myself and asked Sai Baba why he was doing this and pleaded him not to touch my feet. He gave me a reply saying that he was only doing my purification which is very essential to become a pure medium for healing others. I could not stop crying after that which went on till the entire initiation finished. I shared this experience with my reiki teacher and he too was overwhelmed listening to my experience but was definitely not surprised. To the skeptics and intellects this will appear to be my imagination but it happened so abruptly and spontaneously that I had no time to imagine or think and it was not just at the mind level because I felt Sai Baba's touch on my feet, I could feel the water when he was dipping and washing my feet in it. It was no doubt a very real experience for me. Another reason why I would say it was not my imagination or an act of ego gratification, because it did not make me feel good in the beginning and I could have changed my imagination instantly if it was in the control of my mind.

5. Other clairvoyant experiences

Everyday practicing different forms of healings and meditations activated my clairvoyant abilities and I could see and hear lot of things which a normal person would not be able to in its day to day life. But I refrained from sharing this with others because I knew these siddhies or powers are temporary & just a passing phase and my spiritual goal was to go beyond all this and achieve my inner freedom/liberation.

So it was very important for me not to get stuck playing with these toys. These experiences were only there to strengthen my faith and for my inner healing & purification.

An example of such an experience is when I was in one of the shivirs of my guru Avdhoot Baba Shivananda and I saw lots of devi & devtas (divine beings) surrounding the hall from above and showering flowers on us and a few minutes later my guru also revealed the same fact to everyone. If this was my mind imagination then babaji would not have given the exact version of what I was seeing. How could we both see the same thing at the same time? I could see this vision with both my eyes open.

The only time I remember disclosing some facts with others was when I was initiating people into reiki and while initiating them I would see visions which I felt must be shared with those people. One such incident was, when I was initiating one of the students, and with my both eyes open I saw Lord Krishna standing beside the student and giving blessing while the initiation was going on. After sometime when the initiation was over I asked my student if she had any connection with Lord Krishna. She was very surprised to hear that from me and told me that she was a believer of Lord Krishna and had been chanting Krishna mantra for many years. I described to her what I had seen during the initiation and hearing that she had tears in her eyes realizing how much grace and blessings she had received. Once again from the point of view of all the skeptics and intellects, if I was imagining this then I would have seen Lord Shiva and not Lord Krishna because I was a believer of Shiva & secondly I had no clue that she was a believer or devotee of Lord Krishna.

I also had many such experiences with different forms of god and goddesses like Kali, Durga, Lord Shiva, etc in their most beautiful and rudra(fierce) forms, while I was doing shiv & shakti sadhna/meditation.

6. Meeting with a shakti sadhak/upasak

This was in the year 2004 when I was living all alone in Noida, India. While doing different forms of healing practices for others, there was a time when I got very sick with very high fever. I had severe throat congestion and body ache also. In spite of taking many medicines, I was not getting healed completely. My body was becoming very weak and I felt I had no energy left and could die anytime. During this time my healer friend Achla took me to meet one of her friends who was an educated and qualified shakti sadhak/upasak (a devotee of any goddess or female deity). After seeing my condition he suggested me to chant some mantras which included Hanuman chanting (Hanuman is one of the male deities worshipped in Hindu religion) and Durga kavach chanting. He for the first time introduced me to shakti sadhna/meditation invoking the shakti/energy of Durga. (Durga is one of the female deities or goddesses worshipped in Hindu religion). When I asked him the reason for it he said he could sense some external negative entities attacking me, sucking and draining out my energy and in the process making my aura weak. That was not the time for me to rationalize or analyze all of that but to do as he said and see what happens. So with utmost faith and surrender I started to chant the mantras as he had asked me to. After a period of 5 to 10 days my health started improving and my body gained the strength back. I deeply thanked the shakti sadhak for all his help. There was one thing I realized from all this that worship & respect of divine mother or supreme energy/shakti (form & formless dimension) was as important as the divine father or supreme consciousness/shiv (form & formless dimension).

7. Dealing with my family and society

When I made the decision of leaving everything including my job at Indiamart and pursue the path of liberation, it was not easy in the beginning to deal with my whole joint family, who tried their very best to convince me to change my decision. They played all their tactics of emotional blackmailing, trying to make me feel guilty but in the end nothing worked on me because by then I had become fearless and had developed a very strong heart and mind. Gradually everyone stopped saying anything to me as long as I stayed at home and did my sadhna/ meditation instead of going to ashrams. I had no problem staying at home and doing my sadhna/meditation and seva/ selfless work. After a period of three years with lot of my healing, sadhna/meditation, tapasya/austerities and grace of god, my family' s whole attitude completely changed towards me and my path. They became very positive and eventually also started taking guidance from me in personal and spiritual matters.

8. Doing havan for family land/building

Those were the times when my family was going through some financial problems so they came to me for help. There was a big family land which was already constructed in a form of a building but was not getting sold or rented and it was lying vacant for many years. My family wanted this property/land to be given on rent to some big agency or company. I suggested my family to get a havan (votive ritual) done on the land/ building for purification. They all agreed and we called the pandit/priest to do the havan on one of the auspicious days. The place where we did the havan/votive ritual was a big hall. When the havan/votive ritual started, we saw at least 50 to 100 birds coming from outside & sitting inside the hall area making

(129)

lot of noise (chirping). I could sense and see in the subtle dimension that the whole building had at least 50 earth bound souls, entities who were stuck there. I immediately started the process of ascension of entities and spirits taught to us by our guru along with the chanting of mahamrityunjaya mantra mentally. By the time I completed the process, all the earth bound souls and entities had disappeared or rather ascended to higher dimensions. The havan/votive ritual also got over by then and we all witnessed that the birds were no longer making any noise and were leaving the hall. Everyone experienced deep silence & peace. Exactly after 2 months of this havan/votive ritual, this empty building was given on rent to a big & renowned company called Unicef. From there on my family's faith in my spiritual practices strengthened even more.

9. Proving the astrologers wrong and creating my own destiny

Many famous and well known astrologers predicted my future after reading my hand and janampatri/astrological birth chart and said that I would not be able to do my graduation or higher studies, will only be able to study till class 12th, will definitely get married at the age of 26 and have children, will have a major accident or near death experience at the age of 28. None of these things happened because I never believed in what these astrologers said. I did my graduation in arts and did my higher studies and completed my M.B.A specialization in human resource management, never got married and never had any accident where I nearly died. If you are a sadhak (one who follows spiritual teachings and practices meditation), you can change the course of your sanchit karma or dissolve the negative sanchit karma of the past and change your future. (To know more about karma you can read my article on theory of karma)

10. How did I get my spiritual name Shashwati?

I had gone to Tirunamalai with some sadhaks/spiritual seekers as I had heard a lot about Ramana Maharishi's presence in that place who was a spiritual guru and an enlightened being. It was no doubt a wonderful experience being in Ramana's ashram and meditating in one of the caves at the top of the hill. The next day we went to the other ashram next to Ramana's ashram and met a swami ji (spiritual or religious teacher) there. He was giving a discourse and we sat down to listen to him. After the discourse I had a long discussion with him on different aspects of spirituality. We thanked him and as we were leaving he called me and asked me my name. I told him my name is Rachna. Hearing that he very intensely and with lot of force told me, "From now on if anybody asks you your name, tell them that it is Shashwati, as Shashwat means eternal." I accepted it as the divine message and this is how I got my spiritual name Shashwati.

11. Meditation on darkness

Since my childhood I have been a night person, meaning more alert awake and conscious in the night. Would enjoy the silence of the night and I could concentrate better in the night. That is why I did most of my studies in the night. Once I was reading a book of Osho and in that book he talked about meditating on the darkness, where he compared darkness with death. So I sat down in meditation and started meditating on the darkness which was outside and within me. I felt extremely fearful in the beginning and prayed to the spiritual masters to help me go through this process, as I was ready and prepared to face anything. I continued my meditation and kept on going deeper and deeper into this darkness. As I kept going deeper and deeper, I suddenly felt the flow of divine grace and everything within me became very still and silent. I had entered the samadhi (deep trance) of darkness which was very dark, deep, still and silent. I stayed in this state for 2 to 3 hours and then I went into deep sleep.

Chapter Three: My guru Avdhoot Baba Shivananda and the experiences I had because of his shakti/energy, grace and blessings

I called my guru babaji and he made us do lot of sadhna/ meditation, seva/selfless work & sankirtan (singing devotional hymns or songs) for inner cleansing and purification. Sometimes babaji would make us do sadhna/meditation the whole night in his Lucknow ashram. Through his shaktipat (energy transmission) & different techniques/processes of sadhana/ meditation, my mind could release all the negative thoughts & emotions & became more stable, balanced & peaceful.

In most of the babaji's shivirs (spiritual retreats /camps) he would make us do lot of release of negative psychic impressions, blocks, conditionings, negative emotions (fear, anger, pain, trauma, sadness, etc) stored in our subconscious and unconscious mind. He would also make us go through the process of forgiveness, unconditional love and gratitude. The experience was always blissful. I was initiated into Mahamrityunjaya mantra sadhna/meditaion, Shrividya mantra sadhna/meditation, Nachiketa sadhna/meditation, Prati prasav sadhna/meditation.

Doing my sadhna/meditation and seva/selfless work and by maintaining long periods of maun/silence, very soon I reached a state of vairagya (total detachment & desirelessness), with only one desire left for mukti or liberation, which became very intense.

(133)

1. First meeting with my guru Avdhoot Baba Shivananda

When I went for the course of Past Life Regression Therapy conducted by Dr Sunny Satin from California Institute of Hypnosis in the year 2005, I met my guru for the first time as he was one of the participants there. He introduced himself as Rajendar Ratra. We were a group of 12 to 15 people and at that time I did not know that this man named Rajendar Ratra was not an ordinary man but a guru and a realized soul. There was no doubt that he had an amazing presence. He used to be dressed in kurta pajama (Indian dress) and he would talk about his wife and children and his issue of overweight and would make everybody laugh. Obviously he had come as a disguise not wanting anyone of us to know that he was a spiritual guru. We did all the three levels together of 10 days each, so we were almost together for a month. Then we also did the Crystal Healing course together for 2 to 3 days again taught by Dr Sunny Satin. One thing was very strange that most of the participants kept changing in different levels but he and I remained together. He indirectly gave me lot of messages which I did not understand then due to my impure intellect, impure mind and ego, but I did understand its meaning later in my life. For example once while sitting next to me, he made a drawing on a piece of paper and told me that shiv (consciousness) is waiting for the shakti (energy) to rise. On another occasion he asked me what should one do if they have attained mukti/liberation and I replied saying "In that case they should help others to attain the same state". Then he replied saying that he is already doing that. There were few other such messages he gave me but I could not understand the deeper meaning of it then but I did understand the depth of it later in my life.

Another incident which happened during the course was, when I was sitting next to babaji and he had just bought a book on indigo children for his children to read. Then I had asked him if I could borrow this book from him for a day and return it to him next day in the class. He said that he cannot give it to me since his children were eagerly waiting for the book. I told him that it is fine but in my mind I thought that if he really wanted he could have easily given it to me for one day. After a few seconds of having this thought I saw him putting the book in my folder and when I looked at him with amazement, he just smiled at me and said "keep it " as if he just read my thought.

After the course finished we all said goodbyes to each other and I was still not aware of the fact that my guru had actually came to meet me.

2. Two months of silence & search of my guru

In the year 2005 I left my job to get more time and energy to work towards my spiritual goals. Meanwhile I also did divine healing practices for many people. I also read many spiritual books which satisfied me intellectually & apart from that I also got all the knowledge & gyan I needed. Then in the year 2005-2006 I reached a point of frustration where I had all the gyan & knowledge but no deep spiritual experience or samadhi experience (deep trance). I longed for it & my search began. I left my job and my rented house in Delhi, & went to Rishikesh to be in silence for 2 months in Swami Rama's ashram. While in silence, my mind felt an explosion of energy & I went through intense fear, pain & sadness. I felt totally helpless. This was the most traumatic & negative state of my mind. While I was going through intense mental turmoil and pain, I was unable to stop my tears. I was sick and tired of this continued crying which had been going on for many days without any reason. I wanted this crying to stop, so once again I intensely prayed to the spiritual masters to stop this if they are listening to me. And that very second my crying stopped, my tears stopped flowing and I felt extremely peaceful. The peace that I experienced in that moment, I had never experienced it before in my entire life. But this experience was only temporary, as it only lasted for a few hours after which my mental agony again started and I did not know what to do. When I reached the peak of helplessness, I for the first time felt the need of the physical guru who could help me get through this & show me the way. So my search for the guru began.

I prayed very intensely to god to help me find my guru & very soon, while I was meditating I saw a clear image of babaji (Avdhoot Baba Shivananda). Till then I was not aware that the person named Rajendar Ratra whom I had met before during the course of Past Life Regression Therapy was actually Avdhoot Baba Shivananda ji. For me he was only Rajendar Ratra till then. I inquired about him and found out that he is a realized and enlightened soul, and he is also a guru (spiritual teacher), currently giving guru deeksha (initiation) to many people. It came as a shock to me, and suddenly I remembered all the messages he had given me during the course and then I could understand the meaning of all those messages very clearly. By now my mind and intellect had purified enough and my ego was shattered and brutally beaten. I knew in my heart that he was my guru and I took a sigh of relief.

Finally I found my guru in the form of Avadhoot Baba Shivananda & took Shrividya mantra deeksha (initiation) from him in the year 2006, in the month of July.

I also realized that all the painful and negative experiences was a beating and thrashing of the ego to make it so helpless that it finally surrenders to god/guru. All this time I was being purified and prepared to meet my guru so that I can completely surrender at his feet and obey his commands without questioning him or doubting him.

3. Experience of emptiness and detachment

As you know every psychic impression and memory is recorded in the subconscious mind of the child, so when I did Release sadhna/meditation (Prati Prasav sadhna/meditation) with my guru (spiritual teacher/guide) in the later years of my life, he made us release all the psychic impressions of the past from the time I was born up till that day. During the release process/meditation I could remember the times in my childhood when every year my birthday was celebrated and I would always feel sad and depressed & feel anxiety and fear without knowing the reason why. I could never understand that instead of feeling happy why I was feeling so low, so I would force myself to be happy and superficially pretend to be happy. Later while doing the release sadhna/meditation with my guru, my consciousness went back to the time of my mother's death, when I was born. I felt intense pain, sadness, fear, anxiety and I saw that I was crying and saying this to my mother "Please don't leave me alone, I am very scared, I will die". This impression was very deep in my subconscious and I could then understand why I used to feel so low during my birthday celebrations every year, so I did lot of release sadhna/meditation to release these negative emotions and psychic impressions. I had to release these issues from my subconscious. Besides working on my inner cleansing, there was a higher divine purpose for me to experience all this. It was to create that feeling of emptiness & detachment in my heart so that I could later on explore the deeper spiritual meaning of these very profound experiences of life and death and understand that there is no importance of life and death for the atma because it is beyond both, it is only the body which dies.

4. Experience of consciousness expanding to infinity

In 2007 December shivir (spiritual camp) with babaji (my spiritual teacher/guru) I experienced a spiritual state, where I felt absolutely nothing. I could not even feel any compassion love or happiness or bliss. So I ran to babaji in his cottage and asked him if there was something wrong with me because I was feeling nothing. He said, "Emotions and feelings are very gross & what you are experiencing is a very subtle state, so it's ok". After listening to his reply, I was relieved & there after I could go deeper into this state.

After the shivir/spiritual camp ended I went to babaji again with my intense desire of mukti/liberation/nirvana. I was crying, as I asked him to give me mukti. He then asked me, if I wanted moksha (liberation/nirvana) & bhog (pleasure and happiness in the physical dimension) both or only moksha. I said, "I don't know, you are my guru, you know what is best for me so you tell me". He said, "In that case the answer is THE ULTIMATE". He blessed me and put his hand on my head. After this meeting with my guru I came back to my hometown in Lucknow & went inside my sadhna/meditation room & closed the door. I sat with my eyes closed & suddenly I felt a flow of energy like a water fall hitting the top of my head. It went on for sometime & then my mind & body became absolutely still & silent for few days. I could not move or talk.

This was the experience of my mind consciousness expanding to infinity. It was as if it is getting enlightened & awakened to its full potential.

This was the state of Aham Brahmasmi, "I am that I am" where you feel you are everywhere & in everything.

After this incident, I witnessed hundreds of my past lives in a few seconds, including those lives where I was an animal or a plant. After this the release process continued to happen automatically for 24 hours within me, for many days.

My family was not able to understand my state and forced me to eat & drink & talk which I did very reluctantly. After a few days I came back to my normal state.

5. Experience of unconditional pure love-the source of all creation/creativity

My next experience happened in 2008 December shivir/spiritual camp. The third day of the shivir/spiritual camp I felt and experienced infinite love flowing within me, which was infinitely blissful. I experienced, felt and realized that the whole creation is made out of this pure divine love energy. I felt as if there is nothing but love everywhere and in everything. This went on for many hours & then I prayed to babaji & all the spiritual masters, "This experience is great but I don't want this, I want mukti/liberation, I want this 'I' to dissolve, this "self" to dissolve completely".

6. Experience of shoonya/nothingness and pure consciousness

After the experience of unconditional love and bliss, in the December shivir/spiritual camp of 2008, the next day I experienced the whole creation/existence/cosmos with all its dimensions dissolving within me (within my mind) like an entire building being demolished. This continued for many hours & then there was nothing left, no thought, no feeling, no vision, and no experience of any kind. It was a state of no mind (nothingness, shoonya & emptiness). After this experience, I realized that this cannot be the ultimate state or absolute truth because if it is, then who is this "I" who is watching or witnessing or observing this state of no mind or nothingness so I need to experience that ultimate, which is the absolute state of pure consciousness or pure awareness.

And finally the last day of the shivir/spiritual camp I experienced this state, which was a state of pure consciousness where I experienced myself as pure consciousness or pure awareness or pure being.

7. Art of dying

During the art of dying shivir/camp of babaji I got initiated into the process of dying (not physical death but the death of ego and attachments). To start with I went through the experience of my own death and then later in my life as I continued this process I witnessed the death of my family members, death of my city, my country, death of the whole world, death of the whole cosmos happening in my mind and at the same time released the pain, fear, trauma and sadness associated with death. I could see my attachments dissolving, my ego dying gradually and my mind becoming free and empty. This process did not happen all at once but happened in phases as with time I got more and more mentally and physically prepared for it.

8. Negative attachments and entities

During our many past lives or for that matter even during our one lifetime we create many negative attachments and entities of anger, fear, pain, jealously, hatred, etc due to our own negative reactions. Sometimes due to continuous negative thinking and feeling, these entities (not coming from outside but a part of our own consciousness) become so big and strong that they almost become an individual energy being within us. This is one of the major reasons apart from ego, for many psychiatric and mental problems that people face today. While doing sadhna/meditation every day, I would sometimes see these entities coming on the surface as my consciousness level was very high. I was also able to see these energy beings (created by me unconsciously) using my body to communicate to babaji (my guru) and all other sadguru's/spiritual masters for their mukti/liberation and forgiveness. I would like to share one such experience with all of you. Once while I was doing my sadhna/ meditation, one such negative entity came on the surface and as I was watching and witnessing everything, the entity took complete control of my body and started praying to babaji and other masters, and this is what it said "I know I am very bad and I have done lot of bad things in this life and also my past lives, I seek forgiveness for all that I have done, I did it unknowingly and now I want to be free, please help me, only you can help me, I cannot do it myself." After sometime I felt intense divine grace flowing within me and I felt this entity being dissolved, released and freed forever. I felt very light and peaceful and immensely blissful after this intense release.

9. Experience of contentment and bliss

One day after finishing my sadhna/meditation I came out of my room and felt extreme hunger. I had never felt so hungry in my entire life. This hunger was uncontrollable, so I immediately went to my kitchen to find something to eat. At last I found one apple and cut it into 4 pieces. The moment I put one piece in my mouth I felt some very strong force pushing me to go towards my entrance gate. I went out and reached my main entrance gate and saw three children coming towards me. They told me that they were very hungry and wanted something to eat. So I saw in my plate and there were exactly three pieces of apple there and gave one to each of them. I asked them to wait so that I can get something more for them to eat and I rushed inside to get some more food for them. But by the time I returned they had gone. After this whole experience I felt so full and contented with no trace of hunger and felt extreme bliss and ecstasy for many hours. This also made me realize that when you want something very badly for yourself but still you give that to others being totally selfless, you receive lot of divine/god's grace and blessings.

10. Experience of deep samadhi after doing Mahamrityunjaya beej mantra sadhna

I had recently attended one of the shivirs/spiritual camps of babaji (my guru) and was in a very intense & high energy state. I sat down for my sadhna/meditation and felt intense desire to do Mahamrityunjaya beej mantra sadhna/meditation. I did this meditation with lot of intensity and surrender to my guru. Within 20 minutes of doing this sadhna/meditation, I felt intense flow of divine grace. It was so much that I felt my whole body surrounded with this intense divine energy. For some time I could not even feel my body, rather I only felt this energy carrying me, and soon I went into deep silence and stillness. I was unable to move and talk for a very long time.

11. Experience of stillness and silence

Another very deep samadhi/deep trance and flow of grace I experienced, when I was sitting in my small garden in front of my house. My mind was empty with no thoughts at this point and I kept gazing at a beautiful flower in front of me. This went on for a long time and suddenly I felt some energy force hitting the top of my head. I felt this warm flow of energy entering every part of my brain and I no longer could keep my eyes open. So I closed my eyes and everything again became very still and silent within me. I stayed in this state for many hours.

12. My experience in Somnath temple

After attending one of babaji's shivirs/spiritual camp in Somnath I went to visit the famous Somnath temple and a strong urge arose within me to do shiv abhishekam (hindu ritual to worship lord shiv) there. So I contacted one of the priests there and he explained to me the whole procedure. I immediately agreed to him and we planned the abhishekam for next day in the morning, inside the temple. The next morning, the priest started the process with some rituals and chanting and then the process of abhishekam began where I had to chant the shiv mantra and pour flowers, milk, water, etc on the shiv lingam. While I was doing this I could literally see the smiling face of my guru instead of the shivlingam and it felt like I was pouring the milk, flowers, etc on him. I have no words to describe what it felt like. The place I was standing was very small and crowded with other visitors and while I was doing the abhishekam, there was a man standing next to me pushing me from the side all the time, trying to distract my attention. The first 2 times I ignored, then the third time I could not hold myself and told him to maintain his distance from me. But he kept on pushing me and distracting me. I then decided that I would not let anyone distract me during this very sacred process and ignored him completely. After the abhishekam was over, I went back to my room and sat in meditation. While I was meditating I saw the face of the same man and realized he was no ordinary soul but a siddha (spiritual master) who had come to test me. Though I passed in my test of not getting distracted and doing the abhishekam with all my devotion, but tears started flowing from my eyes remembering myself being a little rude to that stranger. I immediately asked for forgiveness in my meditation and felt very light and blessed.

13. My experience in Dattatreya temple in Girnar

After the shivir/spiritual camp in Somnath, I stayed on for another 2 days while all other sadhaks/spiritual seekers left. Somebody had told me about this Dattatreya temple in Girnar which is just 2 hours from Somnath, so I decided to go there alone. The next day evening I took a train for Somnath. The train got a little late so instead of me reaching at 8 pm, I arrived at Girnar station at 10 pm. Girnar is a very small place surrounded by jungles from all sides. I did not know anybody there so I took an auto and told auto driver that I wanted to go to the Dattatreya temple. He told me that the temple is up the hill and will only open next morning around 4 am. So he suggested I take some rest during the night. He took me to a few guest houses but all of them refused to let me stay there saying that I was a single girl so they cannot allow me to stay.

So after searching everywhere and getting no place to stay, the auto guy suggested that I go back to Somnath taking a bus or taxi. I just closed my eyes for few seconds and intensely prayed to the spiritual masters and my guru that I have come to visit the temple and will not go back, so now it is up to them to find a place for me to stay in the night. After finishing my prayer I asked the auto guy to take one more round and see if something can be arranged. He agreed, so while taking the round again, this time an old man called me, who had refused me earlier and told me that, I could stay in his guest house in the night. I was surprised and thanked the spiritual masters and babaji for it. The next morning at 4 am I was all ready to climb up the ten thousand steps, up the hill to reach the Dattatreya temple. I had just started to climb the stairs when I felt a lot of pain in my whole body. I touched my forehead and realized I had very high fever and there was no place nearby where I could find some medicine. The hill I was climbing had deep forest on both sides so nothing was available. I decided to continue no matter what, realizing that I was being tested. After sometime, it started raining heavily but there was no shade so I had no choice but to get wet. My fever and body ache became worse, but I kept moving on. My body was now getting tired and weak, and it was also getting difficult for me to breathe. I could no longer move so I just sat down for some time. While I was sitting two men came towards me with a wooden carriage and asked me if I needed any help. I told them that I had fever and body ache and it was getting difficult for me to move, so they suggested I sit in the carriage. I agreed and they took me half the way. After that they asked me if now I would like to try walking myself. I agreed and continued walking taking rest every now and then. I finally climbed the steps and reached the temple. I meditated there for some time and by 3 pm I was asked to leave as there were no arrangements to stay up there and everyone had to come down before it gets dark. The whole path had no lights so after getting dark they don't allow people to move up and down the hill. I immediately started my journey down the hill. While climbing the steps down it was now even more painful for my body and specially my legs. The pain was becoming unbearable so I kept praying for help and strength. After sometime I could not bear the pain anymore and started crying. There was a small tea shop nearby, I went there and told him my state. He encouraged me and gave me a cup of tea to drink. I thanked him, paid for the tea and started my journey down again. After some more time, I literally gave up as it was getting very difficult for my legs to move. I was feeling very week because of the fever. I sat down crying again. Then two men from nearby village came and asked me why I was crying. I told them the whole story and they said that they would help me climb down. They seemed to be nice and I really needed help so I accepted. I kept both my hands on their shoulders and with their help I started climbing down. They kept encouraging me, though still it was very painful and traumatic but it finally happened and I climbed down. I deeply thanked them for all their help and support. Then I bought a stick for myself to walk. I finally took the auto who took me to the railway station where I had to catch a train for Lucknow. By now I had very high fever, congestion in my throat and lungs, body ache and deep pain in my knees. I was sitting on a bench on the railway platform and suddenly I saw a coolie coming towards me to carry my luggage. But I told him that the train has still not arrived so he has to wait. He agreed and got me a cup of tea realizing that I was not feeling well. I asked him if he could also get some medicine and glucose for me, which he agreed and got it for me very quickly. I took the medicine and drank my tea and felt little better. Meanwhile the train also arrived. Coolie kept my luggage in the compartment and asked me if I needed anything else. I said no and thanked him. I asked him, how much I had to pay him, and in reply he said there was no need to pay anything. I was shocked as I had never heard any coolie saying anything like this to me in the past. He seemed very divine to me. I told him that it was not possible for me to take his services for free so I gave him the amount I felt he deserved. He took the money and left. Throughout this experience I was tested and finally I was given the help I needed by the divine forces or god. It took almost two months for my legs to heal after this event but I know it was a real tapasya (going through real test of austerities).

14. Last meeting with my guru in the physical dimension

I had this strong urge to meet my guru for the last time and ask him my final question. I got this opportunity in Chennai shivir/camp in November 2011 where the organizer who had organized the shivir/camp gave me the permission to meet babaji personally. As always my guru looked at me and smiled and then I asked him, "In my current state which is there for most of the time, I don't feel anything, there is no thought, no desire, cannot do any sadhna, nothing happens, there is only silence. Since last one year I am in this state so what is it". He said, "it is a state of shoonya (nothingness)". I asked him further "What do we call this state?, is it moksha/nirvana, is it self-realization?". He replied, "It is infinite, there is no need to label infinite".

Chapter Four: Important lessons and realizations I had on my spiritual path

1. Learn to say no

This was a lesson I learnt when I was in my teens. I had this problem of saying yes to everything, in other words I could never say no to anyone. I would do all the things everyone asked me to do. Most of the times I liked doing it because pleasing others gave me lot of happiness and satisfaction but there were few times when I really did not like it but yet I did it. During this phase of my life I read a book with the title "Learn to say no when you don't want to say yes". After reading this book I realized what I was doing to myself or my ego. I was allowing people to take advantage of me (my ego) against my wish. I soon learnt this lesson and started applying in my life. Though it was difficult in the beginning to change this habit but still I did it because I realized it was for my own good. People around me got little unhappy seeing this change within me since they were so used to my saying yes to them all the time. It was difficult for them to hear the word "no" from me but with time they understood and got used to it. Since that time I felt internally free to say what I wanted to and at the same time was also able to release the fear of hurting and displeasing others for saying no to them.

2. Purpose of my existence

Next realization happened, when I was getting repeated suicidal thoughts during my teenage years and wanted to end my life. But every time I tried to commit suicide I failed as if there was some strong force protecting me. During these days

I was getting strong thoughts regarding what was the purpose of my existence and what will happen when I die. To know more about it I read a few spiritual books which gave me great insight and clarity. I realized that even if my physical body dies, my other subtle bodies will still exist, my mind will still exist and I will have to take another life and go through the same situations again and again till I dissolve and finish all my sanchit karma, till I resolve all my unresolved issues, till I fulfill or go beyond all my desires, and be liberated while living. This was the first time I realized that how stupid I was to think of ending my life, as god has given me a great opportunity to work out all my karma and make myself free in this life itself, in other words to attain moksha/nirvana/liberation/ultimate freedom in this very life.

3. Achievements and ego

Another realization happened during my student years. I was very hard working by nature. But few students around me who were not that hard working always got more marks than me in all the examinations. So one day I asked the spiritual masters and Shirdi Sai Baba, "Why was this happening to me?" I got an intuitive reply in my meditation. I realized all this was happening for my good, because there was always a possibility for my ego to become big with these achievements. All this was nothing but a beating of my ego. Once I realized this I felt very peaceful and from there on I never bothered about results, only focused on giving my 100% in whatever I did. I also realized the importance of enjoying whatever I did and be happy doing it rather than worrying about the results.

4. Testing the masters

The third lesson I learnt when I was around 19 years old and doing kriya yog meditation inside my room. During this phase of my life I was deeply connected to Paramhansa Yogananda as he was one of the masters of kriya yog path. At that point in my life I was going through some very difficult times and was very upset with all the spiritual masters, sadguru's and Yogananda. So one day when I could no longer hold myself I prayed to all of them with all my intensity. I said in my prayer, "If you all actually exist, show me a sign of your existence or else I will never talk to you all again." As soon as I finished saying this, the electricity (all the three phases) went off in the whole of my neighborhood. I went out of my house and checked everywhere and there was no electricity anywhere. But the most astonishing part was that when I came back to my room, the light of the electric frill in my meditation area was still on for a very long time. I could not believe it and ran out to call my mom to show it to her but the moment she entered my room the light of the electric frill in the meditation area went off. That moment I realized and understood that this experience was only meant for me because I tested the spiritual masters and they gave me a proof of their existence. This whole episode taught me that if you very sincerely, honestly and fearlessly ask for something from the spiritual masters and sadguru's or even your living guru, you will be given!

5. Test by the siddhas

Once I was coming back from my friend s house in Delhi and was about to start my scooter when suddenly from nowhere, a very dark and tall women appeared in front of me. She asked me for some money to feed her hungry children.

Since I was in a hurry I did not pay much attention to her but to gain my attention she continued pleading and begging for some money and told me that she was in a trouble as her husband does not give her any money and beats her. I still was not much moved by her story and told her to complain to the police about it. After that I left from there. But the moment I left I realized what I did was wrong and I should have helped her, so I immediately turned my scooter back and went to the same place. It must have taken me just a couple of minutes to return to that place but by then that woman had gone. I could not believe this so I searched for her everywhere but she was nowhere to be seen. So eventually I returned home and sat down in meditation. During meditation I realized she was no ordinary woman but a siddha (realized soul) who had come to test me and I failed in my test. Realizing this I cried for a very long time and asked for forgiveness from the spiritual masters & siddhas (realized souls) and promised them that I will never make this mistake again.

Very soon I was tested again but this time I was more conscious and aware. A very hideous looking female came to me for the healing and past life regression. She was continuously smoking and I found her very repulsive. But this time I remembered that we should not judge anyone and give unconditional love to all. I did healing and regression for her but nothing seemed to work on her, so I just made her relax and did whatever healing I could do at that time. When she left, I sat down in meditation and I knew that I had passed my test. I felt lot of unconditional love flowing from my heart towards that woman and towards the entire planet earth. I felt very blissful.

6. To have absolute and complete surrender and faith

Once when I was returning from the Shrividya deeksha shivir/initiation camp of my guru in july 2006, in Delhi. I suddenly felt a very strong urge to go to Shirdi Sai Baba temple nearby. So I visited that temple and while I was coming out of the temple, lot of children started coming towards me and begging me to buy an ice cream for them. So I went to the nearby ice-cream vendor and told him to give ice cream to all of them. I suddenly saw more and more children started coming and seeing that it made me a little anxious because I had very little money with me. I also needed some money to take an auto and go back home. Sensing my anxiety the ice cream man said something to me which I can never forget in my entire life. He told me that "why do you worry, nothing is yours, it is his and he is the doer not you", pointing at Sai Baba. Listening to him I felt so ashamed and embarrassed and immediately realized my mistake. All my anxiety and fear was now gone. Having complete faith in Sai Baba and my guru, I told him to continue giving ice creams to all the children. After paying him the money for all the ice creams, I checked the remaining money in my purse, and to my surprise I saw that I was left with the exact amount of money that I needed to take an auto and go back home. I realized and learnt the lesson of having complete surrender and absolute faith towards guru and god for everything in life.

7. Subtle and different forms of ego and egoic mind

Another very big realization I had when I was reading the book "Stillness Speaks" by Ekhart Tolle. After reading his book for the first time I understood and realized the very subtle forms of ego or egoic mind. We all know and are aware of the gross

(152)

form of ego like for instance our identity, name, status, family, etc. But I realized that whether it is overconfidence or under confidence, respect or disrespect, praise or criticism, happiness or sadness, victim or victimizer, they are all subtle forms of ego. All the resistance and conflict is a form of ego. All attachments and desires (good or bad, right or wrong) are forms of ego. We will be able to see and recognize this ego in all its gross and subtle forms only when we become more and more conscious and aware of it.

8. The importance of medical treatment and medications along with spiritual healings

Another important lesson I learnt on my spiritual path. This was during the time when I used to get sick and I did not want to take any medicine prescribed by the doctors, as I wanted to get healed only through spiritual healings. Because of this attitude I used to suffer due to my illnesses for a very long time which could have been prevented if I had taken the medication on time for a couple of days. I then realized that subtle healing energies take its own time to heal and sometimes it may take a longer time to come down at the level of the physical body. I realized that it was only a subtle form of my ego resisting taking medicine. I realized that everything is created by the divine mother (shakti/supreme energy) or god including the medicine. If one can see the divine or gods play in everything, then everything becomes simple to understand and accept. Even my guru says that one must take the advice of doctors and take the medicine prescribed by them on this physical dimension along with spiritual healing and sadhna to work out our karma and dissolve negative energy.

9. Going beyond small siddhies/powers to attain the ultimate

Another very important lesson I learnt during those days when I was very intensely making effort to attain my freedom/liberation/moksha. During one of the shivirs/spiritual camps I went to meet my guru in his cottage in Lucknow ashram. I gave him a gift of two books and one crystal. He accepted the books and returned the crystal to me after blessing it and also taught me the sadhna/meditation of mahamrityunjaya beej mantra to practice with the crystal so that I can attain siddhi/power of trikaal darshi (one who can see past, present and future). After receiving this blessing from him, I was very happy. The next day I started the sadhna/meditation which my guru had taught me but could not continue for very long time. I felt as if some force was stopping me from doing it. I closed my eyes and sat in meditation and asked myself, "What will I get becoming a trikaal darshi? I cannot allow myself to get distracted from my path of ultimate freedom/liberation, in order to attain this siddhi of trikaal darshi". I remembered the words of my guru which he had said long time back, that sadhaks/spiritual seekers are first tested by giving them small toys to play with. Only when they pass these tests and when they throw away the small toys, they are given what they are truly seeking, the real and bigger and higher spiritual growth and experiences.

10. Detachment from the physical body of the guru

A very important realization happened to me when I had requested my guru to let me stay with him in his ashram and do seva/selfless service for him. After listening to my request he closed his eyes and went in silence. I did not understand what this silence meant, so when I was at home, I sat down in meditation. In the silence of my meditation I understood intuitively that my guru was trying to tell me, that since I had already detached myself with everybody and everything, now the time has come for me to also detach myself from him and release this attachment towards his body and his form forever. I had to do this to achieve my ultimate inner freedom. Even though it was very painful for me, I realized that it was important for me to do it.

Besides all these lessons and realizations I was made to learn and realize one very major lesson throughout my life which was of forgiving everyone and able to give unconditional love to all including those who hurt me in some way or the other. Throughout my life I did this even though in some situations it was very difficult but I knew by doing it I will purify my heart and I will be able to resolve all the issues of my past lives with these very people.

Part C: Most important spiritual teachings of all my four gurus which I have practiced and applied in my life. This is one of the main reasons for my spiritual growth and progress.

1. Most important teachings of my first guru Shirdi Sai Baba which I have practiced and applied in my life

Here are the teachings of Sai Baba of Shirdi.

Shraddha

'Shraddha' is a Sanskrit word, which roughly means faith with love and reverence. Such faith or trust is generated out of conviction, which may not be the result of any rational belief or intellectual wisdom, but a spiritual inspiration. According to Sai Baba of Shirdi, steadfast love in God is the gateway to eternity

Saburi

'Saburi'; means patience and perseverance. Saburi is a quality needed throughout the path to reach the goal. This quality must be ingrained in a seeker from day one.

Purity

For Sai Baba it was not the purity of the body but inner purity that mattered. No amount of physical and external cleansing would serve any purpose if the man remained impure in mind and heart.

Compassion

Himself an epitome of compassion and love, Sai Baba taught compassion among his disciples. Baba often told his devotees, 'Never turn away anybody from your door, be it a human being or animal'.

Complete Surrender to the Guru

Sai Baba put Guru on a high pedestal of reverence. For him Guru was the profound base of the path of devotion. He asked for complete surrender to the 'Guru'.

Udi

Udi or the sacred ash was produced from the perpetual fire called 'dhuni' lit by Sai Baba in Dwarkamai at Shirdi. Explaining the meaning of life he would refer to Udi and taught that, like Udi all the visible phenomena in the world are transient. Through this example Sai Baba wished to make his devotees understand the sense of discrimination between the unreal and the real. Udi taught the devotees discrimination or vivek.

Dakshina

Sai Baba would demand 'Dakshina' or alms from those who visited him. This explained the sense of non-attachment to worldly things. Hence dakshina taught the devotees non-attachment or vairagya.

2. Most important teachings of my second guru Paramhansa Yogananda which I have practiced and applied in my life

Cosmic consciousness

As a small cup cannot hold an ocean within it, no matter how willing it may be to do so, likewise the cup of material human consciousness cannot grasp the universal cosmic consciousness, no matter how desirous it is; but when the student, by meditation and concentration, enlarges the caliber of his consciousness to omniscience, he can hold the universal consciousness in all atoms.

'Seek ye the kingdom of god first and all these things shall be added unto you.

You are all gods if you only knew it. Behind the wave of your consciousness is the sea of god's presence. You must look within. Don't look at the little wave of the body with its weaknesses but look beneath, close your eyes and you see only the vast omnipresence before you, everywhere you look. You are in the center of that vast sphere and as you lift your consciousness from the body and all its experiences you will find it is filled with the great joy and bliss that lights the stars and gives power to the winds and storms. God is the fountain of all our joys and of all the manifestations in nature.

"God has not to be earned. Seek ye the kingdom of god first and all these things shall be added unto you."

Guru and teacher

It is extremely necessary to remember that in the beginning it is wise to compare many spiritual paths and teachers, but when the real GURU (Preceptor) and the real teaching is found, then the restless searching must cease. The thirsty one should not keep seeking wells, but should go to the best well and daily drink its nectar. That is why in India, in the beginning we seek many until we find the right path, and the right master, and then remain loyal to him through death and eternity, until final emancipation.

One attracts spiritual teachers when he is desirous of spiritual training, but a guru, or direct messenger of god, is sent only when the disciple is extremely determined to know god. God uses the speech, mind, and wisdom of the guru to teach and redeem the disciple.

Tuning in to the will of the guru

The first requisite in your spiritual path lies in finding your spiritual guru who will discipline you and take a personal interest in your spiritual welfare and lead you as far along the spiritual path as you wish to go. Having found him, follow him closely, obey him with devotion, and practice what he teaches you; thus ultimately you will attain your highest goal.

Freedom of will

Very few people truly know what freedom of will means. To be compelled to do things by the dictates of your own instincts and habits is not freedom. To be good because you have been so for a long time and to refrain from evil because you are accustomed to do so is not freedom. When your will is perfectly free to choose good instead of evil anytime, anywhere, because you really feel good then you will know real happiness: then indeed are you free. Evil gives only sorrow. When the influences of heredity, prenatal and postnatal habits, family, social, and world environment, all cease to influence your judgment, when you can act, guided only by your highest inner intuitive discrimination-then only are you free.

Movie drama of life

"When you see a motion picture of a performance on the stage, if you know the play beforehand it will not be so interesting. It is good that you don't understand this life because god is playing a movie drama in your life. It wouldn't be interesting if we knew what was going to happen before it happened. Don't be interested for the end. But always pray to god, 'teach me to play in this drama of life, so that whether I am weak or strong, sick or well, high or low, rich or poor, with an immortal attitude, I may at the end of this drama know the moral of it all.'

The signs of a guru

The signs of a guru are as follows: his eyes are still and unwinking whenever he wants them to be so; by the practice of Yoga his breath is quiet without his forcibly holding it in his lungs; his mind is calm without effort. If a man has eyelids that blink continually and lungs acting like bellows all the time, and a mind always restless like a butterfly, and he keeps on telling you he is in cosmic consciousness, laugh at him. Just as sleep manifests in the body by certain physiological changes, so the muscles, eyes, breath, all usually become still during cosmic consciousness.

Surrendering everything to god

Give everything to god, and you will change because then the human ego can no longer dictate to you. No matter what comes to you, just say, "God knows best. It is He who is giving me this suffering; it is He who is making me happy." With this attitude, all your nightmares of life will change into a beautiful dream of god.

Gods cosmic dream movie

You can understand life as god's cosmic dream movie if you analyze the dream movies you create every night in sleep. Sometimes you have nightmares and sometimes you have lovely dreams. How real they seem, not only to you but also to those beings in your dream. But when you wake up you know that they were not real, and you can laugh at that unreality. But if you will see and think of a dream as a dream, whether it is enjoyable or dreadful, you will have peace. When you realize that life is a dream, then you are free. So remember, god is dreaming this world. And if we are in tune with Him, we will live a divinely intoxicated life and nothing will disturb us. We will watch this cosmic picture as we watch the films in a movie house, without being hurt.

Act according to the inner direction

First find out what you want; ask divine aid to direct you to right action, whereby your want will be fulfilled; then retire within yourself. Act according to the inner direction that you receive; you will find what you want. When the mind is calm, then how quickly, how smoothly, how beautifully will you perceive everything.

A few guidelines

Let half of your diet be raw food. Eat more ground nuts, rather than too much meat. Don't indulge in very hot or cold drinks. Thus you will avoid catching cold. Drink more orange juice. Omit lunch or dinner as often as you can (whenever you are not hungry). Fast one day a week. Run every day or take a very brisk walk. Help in hospital and prison and other welfare work. Do your daily work cheerfully, intensely, seeking more opportunities so that you may serve more and more members of the human family. Don't criticize anyone except yourself.

Daily deep efforts of meditation, can get you to the divine goal. To reach god you must get away from crowds, get away from too many distractions, too many movies, too many fruitless engagements, too many desires, too much waste of time, too many blind and hypocritical commercial teachers.

Use the night hours as much as you can, and the early morning, and all gaps between demanding duties, to inwardly pray with your soul to god, "Reveal thyself." Solitude is the price of god-realization.

Facing difficulties with faith and being fearless

There is no difficulty that cannot be solved, provided you believe you have more power than your troubles, and you use that power to shatter your impediments. If you live with the consciousness that you are working for god alone; you have left everything for his cause, you are his child and that he is your father, and you make up your mind to do your best with dogged determination, then in spite of obstacles, and even if you make mistakes, his power will always be there to help you out. I live by that law. If you can go through your tests smiling with faith in god, and without harboring any doubts, you will see how god's law works.

Use the law of meditation. It is the law of all laws, for it brings response from the supreme power behind all power. That supreme power will work for you as it has always worked for me.

The best time to pray

The time to pray to god for guidance is after you have meditated and felt that inner peace and joy; that is when you pray as you have made divine contact. It is a fact that sometimes your most fervent prayers and desires are your greatest enemies. Talk sincerely and justly with god, and let him decide what is right for you. If you are receptive, he will lead you, he will work with you. Even if you make mistakes, don't be afraid. Have faith. Know that god is with you.

Life is a matrix of consciousness

We are made of the matrix of consciousness. All life was spumed out of the one source of the river of consciousness. Your individualized consciousness is thus the very foundation of your existence. All of your thoughts and actions are bubbles and droplets of the river of consciousness. The seemingly solid body is actually a mass of electromagnetic currents. Its electrons and protons are condensations of the relative positive and negative creative thoughts projected by god, which I call thoughtrons. All creation comes from these thoughtrons, the consciousness of god.

In the ultimate sense, then, all things are made of pure consciousness,- their finite appearance is the result of the relativity of consciousness. Therefore, if you want to change anything in yourself, you must change the process of thought that leads to the materialization of consciousness into different forms of matter and action. That is the way, the only way, to remold your life.

Discrimination and will power

Both discrimination and will power are necessary. Remolding your consciousness means exercising free will guided by discrimination and energized by will power. Discrimination is your keen eyesight and will is your power of locomotion. Without will power, you may know what is right through discrimination and yet not act on it. It is acting on knowledge that gets you to your goal. So both discrimination and will power are necessary.

Probing the core of nervousness

Desire and attachment feed the disease of nervousness. By the time you have acquired the things you crave, you are worn out. Desirelessness and nonattachment is freedom from the tyranny of enslavement to possessions

Errors in judgment are a result of not having developed intuition

Errors in judgment are a result of not having developed intuition. Most of you have had the feeling that you could be great, and do great things; but because you have lacked intuitive power, that potential has, for the most part, remained dormant. To progress and to avoid the misery of mistakes, you have to find what is the truth in everything. This is possible only if you develop your intuition. By not developing the faculty of intuition, you make wrong decisions, pick up the wrong business associates, and get caught up in wrong personal relationships. Since the judgment of your mind is conditioned by the information fed to it by the senses, if your senses become deluded you may think a person is wonderful without knowing what he truly is inside. You may think you have found your soul mate, so you enter into matrimony and then end up in the divorce court. But intuition will never make such a mistake. It will not look at the magnetic power of the eyes or at the attractive face or personality of a person, but will feel and perceive accurately in the heart what that person is really like. If you use your intuition, you will know the very purpose for which you exist in this world and when you find that, you find happiness.

To work for god is to be free.

Those who cling selfishly to their wealth instead of doing good with it do not attract prosperity in their next life. They are born poor, but with all the desires of the wealthy. But those who share their good fortune attract wealth and abundance wherever they go. If you learn to share with others, you will see that god is ever with you,- He will never leave you. Depend upon Him, and He will look after you. Do not forget that your very life is directly sustained by the power of god. When you remember that your reason, will, and activity are dependent upon Him, you will be guided by god, and you will realize that your life is one with His infinite life. To work for yourself is to be bound by life. To work for god is to be free.

Spiritualizing ambition with the ideal of service

Business is nothing but serving others materially in the best possible way. Those stores that start out with the idea of only making money are readily recognized as commercial money-making dens. But stores that concentrate on serving customers with the best articles at the minimum cost will succeed and also advance the moral development of the world.

Do not be a doormat

There is a time to remain quiet but firm. In your efforts to get along with others, do not be a doormat or else everyone will want to run your life for you. If they cannot dominate you, they get angry; and if you listen to them and do their bidding, you become spineless. Then how are you supposed to behave? When you find resistance to your ideals, the best way is to just remain quiet but firm. Say nothing. Do not get angry. You may get verbal punch after punch, but do not permit it to provoke you. Refuse to quarrel. Eventually those persons will understand that you do not mean to anger them, but at the same time you have your own good reasons for not wanting to do what they request of you.

Do not sacrifice your ideals to please others

Do not sacrifice your ideals to please others. Getting along with people does not mean agreeing with everybody,- and it does not mean that you should sacrifice your ideals for their sake. That is not the kind of getting along that I mean. But you can maintain your ideals without being offensive. So above everything else, please god and live up to your own ideals; never compromise your ideals, and never harbor an ulterior motive. If you can live loving god and mean no harm to anyone, and still the world wants to hurt you, that is all right. It is better to be cursed by the whole world and be a favorite child of god than to be loved by all and forsaken by god. Getting along with others means getting along first with your conscience and with god, and then with people.

Learn to act wisely by attunement with a true guru

Let every action, be guided by wisdom and never by a desire to hurt anybody. But if anyone is hurt because of your doing the right thing, you should not be afraid; you have to answer to yourself, not to anyone else. Even god is not your judge,- you are your own judge. If you act wrongly, you are going to punish yourself. If you act rightly, you will free yourself. That is the justice of the law of karma. You are dictated neither by god nor by his angels, but by the law of action: What you sow, you reap. Whenever you meet with misfortune, do not put the blame for it on god. The blame rests with you alone—resulting from your past actions.

The right attitude towards suffering

Suffering is a good teacher to those who are quick and willing to learn from it. But it becomes a tyrant to those who resist and resent. Suffering can teach us almost everything. Its lessons urge us to develop discrimination, self-control, nonattachment, and transcendent spiritual consciousness.

Life being a vast school for learning lessons

Life is a vast school. There is a lesson to be learned in everything. Life is teaching you all the time,- you are a bad student if you don't pay attention. Christ, Krishna, Buddha, and all the enlightened ones finished their training, graduated with honors, and went back to god. They don't have to come to this school of life anymore, unless of their own free will they return again as teachers, "saviors," to help others.

Reincarnation means that you did not finish your schooling; you have yet to pass in all the grades of physical, mental, and spiritual unfoldment, which will earn for you a diploma of perfection and freedom.

Turn your trials into triumphs

It is never too late to improve oneself. Watch your thoughts, feelings, and actions, and guide them rightly. At the end of each day, analyze yourself: How have you lived this day? To be really living is to strive constantly to improve oneself; physically, mentally, spiritually. A person who has not become stationary, but continues to change for the better—day after day, year after year—develops magnetism. Use every trial that comes to you as an opportunity to improve yourself. Each test should bring out the hidden power that is within you as a child of god, made in his image.

Put your duties in proper perspective

The teaching of yoga does not advise you to fly away from your duties in the world. It tells you to saturate yourself with the thought of god while you do your part in this world where he has placed you.

Divine love is unsurpassable

If you could but realize the romance that some devotees have with god, you can understand that no other experiences can equal that joy. The moment divine love possesses your heart, your entire body becomes blissfully still.

The power of all powers

Never accept karmic limitations. Don't believe you are incapable of doing anything. Often when you can't succeed at something it is because you have made up your mind that you cannot do it. But when you convince your mind of its accomplishing power, you can do anything! By communion with god you change your status from a mortal being to an immortal being. When you do this, all bonds that limit you will be broken. This is a very great law to remember. As soon as your attention is focused, the power of all powers will come, and with that you can achieve spiritual, mental, and material success.

Your success is what you have attained within

It is what you have attained within that determines your success. If you have attained nothing within, you will have no happiness. And if you have nothing outside, but you are happy within, you will have all success.

When a problem thwarts you—when you find no solution and no one to help you—go into meditation.

When a problem thwarts you—when you find no solution and no one to help you—go into meditation. Meditate until you find the solution

The true signs of progress in meditation are the following:

The true signs of progress in meditation are the following:

• An increasing peacefulness during meditation.

• A conscious inner experience of calmness in meditation metamorphosing into increasing bliss.

• A deepening of one's understanding, and finding answers to one's questions through the calm intuitive state of inner perception.

• An increasing mental and physical efficiency in one's daily life.

• Love for meditation and the desire to hold on to the peace and joy of the meditative state in preference to attraction to anything in the world.

• An expanding consciousness of loving all with the unconditional love that one feels toward his own dearest loved ones.

• To make actual contact with god, and worship Him as ever new bliss felt in meditation and worship Him in His omnipresent manifestations within and beyond all creation.

Having unconditional love for god

If you think of god in deepest meditation, if you love Him with all your heart, and feel completely at peace in His presence, without wishing for anything else, then the divine magnetism of god will attract unto you everything you ever dreamed about, and much more. If you have unconditional love for god, He will drop thoughts in others' brains, so that they become instruments to fulfill even your unspoken desires.

Jealousy

Jealousy comes from an inferiority complex, and expresses itself through suspicion and fear. It signifies that a person is afraid and he cannot hold on his own in his relationships with others, be they conjugal, filial, and social.

Love and its counterparts can never be acquired or preserved by demands or begging or bribes. True love cannot be bought. To receive love, one must give it freely, without any condition. But instead of following this rule, the insecure person resorts to jealousy. This makes the loved one angry, and thus defeats its very purpose. Jealousy then responds to the anger with a desire to strike back. But anytime one wants to harm another, he ultimately hurts himself even more. Successful relationships can grow only in trust and love. Love survives in respect, usefulness, and freedom from possessiveness.

Astrlogical charts and horoscope

It is your will power that is going to determine what you are able to do—nothing else: not your past habits, not your past karma, not your horoscope. Consulting astrological charts gives authority and strength to your past karma. It weakens your will power.

Faith is ever secure—Direct perception of truth

Faith not only produces results in healing or in other successes, it is also the power that reveals the outworking of spiritual laws that underlie all so-called miracles. Belief can be swayed or destroyed by contrary evidence and doubt; but faith is ever secure, because it is direct perception of truth.

Seeking union with god

Seeking union with god by wisdom alone, by devotion alone, or through action alone is one-sided. The far superior way is to take your mind and vital forces and all your desires, and your devotion and wisdom and service, and dissolve them all in god. So, the easiest and best way to god is not to be limited only to Gyana Yoga, Bhakti Yoga, or Karma Yoga, but to combine them.

Why should god amuse us with powers and miracles?

When you truly desire god and you do not crave anything else, including powers then you will not run after powers or miracles. The attainment of the ability to perform miraculous feats is not necessarily an indication that one knows god.

Conversation with god requires silence

Conversation with god requires silence. People who talk too much are not with god; there is much less time in their thoughts for god. Those who inwardly converse with god are outwardly more silent. No matter what their surroundings, they are habitually more quiet. Because the devotee has plenty to say to god, he has very little to say to others. When those who have much to say to god do speak, their words are of god, and are full of wisdom and understanding. Idle talking causes one to lose devotion for god. It feeds mental restlessness that takes the mind away from god.

From this moment on be sincere and fearless in truth

To be a teacher, you must be sincere. Whatever you say, you must feel from within. If you are upright and honest, your spirit can never be bribed to deviate from god's principles. You cannot be unkind because you are not activated by egotism or anger. What you do, you do with the utmost sincerity. Be sincere and fearless in truth from this moment on. Wherever you go, let the lord, not your ego, speak through you. You do not have to be shrewd with people; you have to be genuine. If you are genuine, everyone who is sincere will be harmonious with you— you will receive genuine feeling from them.

Love people, but not their faults

If you love god and therefore love everybody, that does not mean that you love the faults in people.

Attachment

Attachment is disastrous, because it is compulsive and limiting. Disband attachment and learn to give true, sincere love to all. True love is impersonal and is not bound by anything.

Real love versus selfish love

Real love is when you are constantly watching the progress of the soul. As soon as you cater to someone's bad habits, you are not loving that soul anymore. You are just pleasing that person to avoid ill will. Never agree with anyone who is wrong, not even those who are nearest and dearest to you. To agree with wrongdoing is to bribe your soul in order to be looked upon favorably by the wrongdoer, and later on that will come out in some disastrous results.

While there is yet time, meditate!

While there is yet time, meditate! I hope you will all make the supreme effort to meditate. Your search for god cannot wait. Let all else wait, but do not keep god waiting for you. Tarry no more, lest old age and disease suddenly terminate your life. While there is yet time and opportunity, meditate. Be true in your heart. Do not make a display of your devotion for god before others. Be sincere. Be concentrated; be adamant in your effort in meditation, for the almighty is with us.

Recognizing those you knew in past lives

How can you recognize those you knew before? In a crowd of strangers, sometimes there is one towards whom you feel at the very first meeting that you have known him or her long ago. With others you never feel close, no matter how much you associate with them. If you are unhampered by prejudices and you find or come across souls whose faces and personalities draw you much more strongly than others, it is likely that you knew those souls in past lives.

Learn the lesson that you are not a man nor a woman, but a soul made in the image of god

Learn the lesson that you are not a man nor a woman, but a soul made in the image of god. Otherwise, god will have to send you here again and again until you outgrow your ignorance and realize your true self. Become so conscious of god that you know He is the only reality.

If you can retain your inner peace, therein lies your supreme victory. No matter how you are situated in life, never feel justified in losing your peace. When peace is gone and you cannot think clearly, you have lost the battle. If you never lose your peace, you will find you are always victorious, no matter what the outcome of your problems. That is the way to conquer life.

3. Most important teachings of my third guru Osho which I have practiced and applied in my life

Oneness

It is the phenomenon of harmony. It means that two bodies are still two bodies, but the two souls within them are no more two. It is one soul within two bodies: That's exactly the meaning of harmony. It is the most exquisite experience. Harmony means you are dropping your ego and you are saying, "I would like to be with you, so deeply one, that this very idea of `I' is no more needed."

Heart and mind

The disciple who can wait will find all his questions answered at the right moment. But waiting is a great quality: it is deep patience, it is great trust. The mind cannot wait, it is always in a hurry. It knows nothing about patience; hence it goes on piling questions upon questions without getting the answer.

And in the world of the heart there is only the answer, because the heart knows how not to ask, how to wait: The disciple has to understand this whole situation — that the dictatorship of the mind has to be destroyed, that the mind is only a servant, not a master. The master is the heart, because all that is beautiful grows in the heart; all that is valuable comes out of the heart – – your love, your compassion, your meditation.

What is beyond enlightenment?

Beyond enlightenment you enter into nothingness. Experience disappears, experiencer disappears. Just pure nothingness and utter silence remains. Perhaps this is the destiny of every human being, which is to be achieved sooner or later. Beyond enlightenment just as you enter into nothingness, there must be a possibility of coming out of nothingness and go back into form, back into existence — renewed, refreshed, luminous — on a totally different plane. Because nothing is destroyed as things can only go into a dormant state; things can go only into deep sleep. Then in the morning they wake up again.

Mind

The mystics, for thousands of years, have been saying that all these things that your mind is filled with are not yours, you are beyond them. You get identified with them, and that's the only sin.

Desire & gratitude

If you don't understand desire you will go on changing your objects of desire. And the desire will continue to be the same. And you will be in the grip of it. This is a very unconscious state. You are suffering from desire, but you think you are suffering from things. Look into desire. Meditate on desire. Go deep into it. See it as deeply as possible. Layer upon layer, penetrate into it. Penetrate to the very core of it. In that very penetration there comes a renunciation which is not of your making. There comes a renunciation which is a gift. And because it comes out of understanding, you need not cultivate it, you need not practice it. It's very coming is transforming. You go through a mutation.

Remember this. If you start feeling grateful, you will be transformed. You will start changing your being from baser metal into gold – this is what alchemy is all about.

Problems

DO REAL PROBLEMS EXIST?

They exist only when you are unconscious – then they are real. Problems exist if you are not centered, not alert. If you become centered, alert, watchful, a witness, problems simply dissipate, evaporate. Are all problems just mind games? Yes. They are all mind games. And 'mind' is nothing but another name for unconsciousness. Never bring awareness through willpower. Anything brought by will-power is going to be wrong –let that be the criterion. Then how to bring awareness? Understand. When anger comes, try to understand why it has come; try to understand without any condemnation, without any justification either, without any evaluation. Just watch it. You should be neutral. Just as you watch a cloud moving in the sky: similarly in the inner sky an anger cloud moves – you watch it. See what it is. Look deep into it. Try to understand it. And you will find there is a chain: the anger cloud disappears, but because you looked deeply into it, something else has been found – maybe ego was hurt, that's why you became angry. Now watch this ego cloud, which is more subtle. Go on watching it. Get deep into it. Nobody has ever been able to find anything in the ego. So if you go deep into it, you will not find it; and when you have not found it, it is no more. Then suddenly there is a great light – out of understanding, out of penetration, out of witnessing, with no effort, with no will, with no conclusion that it should be like this or should be like that. A neutral witnessing. And awareness arises. And this awareness has beauty and benediction. This awareness will heal you.

Form & formlessness

Attachment to form or to formlessness is the same. I am not giving you a formless god, I am not trying to substitute form by formlessness – no, I want you to drop both form and formlessness and just be… free of all illusions. In that just being is freedom.

Prayer

So the first thing that I can say about prayer is: a feeling of immense gratitude, a thankfulness. Second thing is that Prayer is a way of living. What do I mean? A man of prayer remains in prayer twenty-four hours a day.

What is enlightenment?

Enlightenment simply means an experience of your consciousness unclouded by thoughts, emotions, and sentiments. When the consciousness is totally empty, there is something like an explosion, an atomic explosion. Your whole insight becomes full of a light which has no source and no cause. And once it has happened, it remains. It never leaves you for a single moment; even when you are asleep, that light is inside. And after that moment you can see things in a totally different way. After that experience, there is no question left in you.

Enlightenment means being fully conscious, aware. Ordinarily we are not conscious and not aware. We are doing things either out of habit or out of biological instincts.

When one is enlightened one is conscious, but one is not conscious of consciousness. One is perfectly conscious, but there is no object in it.

Trust

It is only when you can trust the unknown that you can trust a master, never before it, because the master represents nothing but the unknown.

Clarity

Clarity is not part of the mind at all; clarity is the absence of the mind, confusion is the presence of the mind. Confusion and mind are synonymous. You can't have a clear mind. If you have clarity, you cannot have the mind; if you have the mind, you can't have clarity. The mind is always divided against itself, it lives in conflict. Divisibility is its nature.

Humbleness

If you are humble, you are an egoist standing on his head. Humbleness is an expression of the ego. I am neither. I am simply whatsoever I am, neither humble nor egoistic, because I have seen that there is no ego. How can there be humbleness then?.

Love and freedom

Freedom can be willed because it is your own decision to remain in a prison. It is your own responsibility. You have willed your slavery, you have decided to remain a slave, and hence you are a slave. Change the decision, and the slavery disappears. But love cannot be willed. Love is a by-product of freedom; it is the overflowing joy of freedom, it is the fragrance of freedom. First the freedom has to be there, then love follows. If you try to will love, you will create only something artificial, arbitrary. A willed love will not be true love, it will be phony. You cannot be ordered to love somebody, you cannot order yourself to love somebody. If it is not there, it is not there; if it is there, it is there. It is something beyond your will. In fact it is just the opposite of will: it is surrender.

Marriage

Love, and love as deeply as possible. And if love itself becomes the marriage, that is another thing, altogether different. If love itself becomes such an intimacy that it is unbreakable, that is another thing, that is not a legal sanction. Legal sanctions are needed only because you are afraid. You know that your love is not enough; you need the legal support for it. You know perfectly well that you can escape or the woman can escape, hence you need the policeman to keep you together. But this is ugly, to need a policeman to keep you together. That's what marriage is!

Being total

Whatsoever you are learning, learn it in its totality. Don't let it be just a hit-and-run affair, go into it as if it is your whole life. Stake everything! Be total, whatsoever you do, because it is only out of totality that one learns. It is only when you are totally into something that mysteries are revealed to you.

Love and freedom

Man's greatest longing is for freedom. Freedom is the very essential core of human consciousness: love is its circumference and freedom is its center. These two fulfilled, life has no regret. And they both are fulfilled together, never separately. Your freedom and your love have to grow hand in hand, in deep embrace, in a kind of dance, helping each other. And then the total man is born, who lives in the world and is not of the world at all. Just to love without freedom is to be impoverished, or just to be free without love is to live in loneliness, sadness, darkness.

Freedom is needed for love to grow, love is needed so that freedom can be nourished.

Being nothing

The moment you are nothing, you become a door – a door to the divine, a door to yourself, a door that leads to your home, a door that connects you back to your intrinsic nature. And man's intrinsic nature is blissful. You are silent, standing on the door of nothingness; just a step more inwards and you have found the greatest treasure that has been waiting for you for thousands of lives.

Meditation, clarity and witnessing

Meditation is nothing but your mind in a silent state. Just as a lake is silent, not even ripples on it. Thoughts are ripples. Meditation is mind in a relaxed state. Clarity, in its ultimate stage, becomes an explosion of light which we have called 'enlightenment.' It is simply in the intensity of clarity that darkness disappears. It is because you can see so clearly that darkness is no more there. Your insight becomes so penetrating that all darkness is dispelled.

Meditation also means to watch the movement of thoughts in the mind. Just be an observer, as if you are standing by the side of the road watching the traffic – with no judgment, no evaluation, no condemnation, and no appreciation – just pure observation.

Wisdom

When you are able to see with no dust of knowledge on the mirror of your soul, when your soul is without any dust of knowledge, when it is just a mirror, it reflects that which is. That is wisdom. That reflecting of that which is, is wisdom. Knowledge gratifies the ego, wisdom happens only when the ego is gone, forgotten.

Pure being

These are the three things: feeling comes first, then comes thought, then comes the act. You may not be aware at all that each thought is produced by a certain feeling. If the feeling is not there, the thought will not come. Feeling becomes actualized in thought, thought becomes actualized in the act. And if you can be aware of these three things, suddenly you will fall into the deepest core of your being.

Responsibility and gratitude

Drive all blame into one. And that one is you. Once this insight settles: "I am responsible for my life — for all my suffering, for my pain, for all that has happened to me and is happening to me — I have chosen it this way; these are the seeds that I sowed and now I am reaping the crop; I am responsible" — once this insight becomes a natural understanding in you, then everything else is simple. Then life starts taking a new turn, starts moving into a new dimension. That dimension is conversion, revolution, and mutation — because once I know I am responsible, I also know that I can drop it any moment I decide to. Nobody can prevent me from dropping it.

Be grateful to everyone. Because everybody is creating a space for you to be transformed — even those who think they are obstructing you, even those whom you think are enemies. Your friends, your enemies, good people and bad people, favorable circumstances, unfavorable circumstances — all together they are creating the context in which you can be transformed and become a buddha. Be grateful to all.

Surrender and dependency

Surrender is out of love, dependency is out of fear. Dependency is a relationship in which you are hankering for something, desiring something and there is a motive. You are ready to become dependent — that's what you are willing to pay for something. Surrender has no desire in it. It is sheer joy, it is trust, and it is unmotivated. It is like falling in love. Surrender is the highest form of love, the purest form of love. You will not feel dependent, because there will be no clinging in it. You will not feel dependent, because it is not out of loneliness that you have surrendered. If you have surrendered out of loneliness then it is not surrender at all, then it is something else.

Freedom

Freedom means freedom from the mind. Only a no-mind knows the taste of freedom. But to be a no-mind is so risky; you will have to lose all that you have become accustomed to, all that you have become so attached to.

As the ultimate comes, you disappear.

The doors are always open. And the ultimate comes, but you cannot have a glimpse of the ultimate– whether you want to call him 'him' or 'her' does not matter. As the ultimate comes, you disappear. The happening is simultaneous, there is no gap. The moment the ultimate descends, you are already gone. He comes only in the space where you used to be, in your nothingness. Nobody has seen the ultimate, for the simple reason that to see the ultimate you have to disappear, you cannot be a witness. You can become it but you cannot see it. We call those people who have become it the mystics; they are not the ones who have seen God, they have become God. It is not an object for them to see. It is their very subjectivity, it is their very being.

Ego and cowardice

The ego is cowardice. Cowardice is not an essential part of the ego, it is the whole of the ego. And it is bound to be so, because the ego lives in constant fear of being exposed: it is empty within, it is non-existential; it is only an appearance, not a reality. And whenever something is only an appearance, a mirage, the fear is bound to be there at the very center of it. The ego makes you a coward. Egolessness makes you a fearless pilgrim of the eternal mystery of life.

Being nobody

Everybody is afraid of being nobody. Only very rare and extraordinary people are not afraid of being nobody. A Gautam Buddha is needed to be a nobody. A Nobody is not an ordinary phenomenon; it is one of the greatest experiences in life – that you are and still you are not, that you are just pure existence with no name, with no address, with no boundaries… you are neither a sinner nor a saint, neither inferior nor superior, you are just a silence. People are afraid because their whole personality will be gone; their name, their fame, their respectability, all will be gone; hence, the fear.

Being in the world, not escape

Many escape from life just because life is too much, and they don't find themselves capable of coping with it. I will not suggest that; I am not an escapist. I will tell you to fight your way through life, because that is the only way to become more aware and alert; to become so balanced that nobody can unbalance you; to become so tranquil that the presence of the other never becomes a distraction. The other can insult you but you are not irritated. The other can create a situation in which, ordinarily, you would have gone mad, but you don't go mad. You use the situation as a stepping stone for a higher consciousness. Life has to be used as a situation, as an opportunity to become more conscious, more crystallized, more centered and rooted. If you escape, it will be as if a seed escapes from the soil and hides in a cave where there is no soil, only stones. All escape is suicidal.

Going beyond happiness and unhappiness both

If happiness is there, then just beyond it somewhere unhappiness will be present. If unhappiness is there, then somewhere on the boundary happiness will be present. They go together. The evil mind is followed by misery, by hell, but somewhere hell is followed by heaven. The holy mind is followed by happiness, but happiness is followed by unhappiness, because they cannot be separate. They are not two phenomena. How can you be happy if you cannot be unhappy? If you have forgotten what unhappiness is you will forget happiness too. If you don't know what disease is or illness is, you will not be able to feel your health or wellbeing. It is impossible. To keep alert that you are healthy, sometimes illness is a must.

So ultimately the holy mind and the evil mind are not two minds, they are two aspects of the same coin. The saint and the sinner exist together. The saint can turn into a sinner any moment and the sinner can turn into a saint any moment. They are not far away, they are not distant neighbors. They live very close by, they are very intimate. Their boundaries meet and merge.

In the state of no-mind — there is neither saint nor sinner, neither happiness nor unhappiness. The duality is dropped. Then there is silence, serenity. Then there is peace, all turmoil is gone.

Attachment

Now, if you are attached to things, you cannot be a lover. Only a nonattached man can raise himself towards that sky which we call love. Remember, if your nonattachment to things is true and has come out of understanding, has grown out of awareness, you will become more loving. Because the same energy that was involved in attachment will now be released. Where will it go? You will have more energy at your disposal. Attachment is not love. It is an ego trip — to possess, to dominate, to manipulate. It is violence; it is not love. When this energy is relieved, suddenly you have much more energy to love. A really nonattached person is full of love, and always and always he has more and more to give, and always he goes on finding new sources of love.

Diplomacy

Diplomacy is a beautiful name for all kinds of cunningness.

A spiritual person has to drop all diplomacy. He has to be authentic, sincere; he has to be as he is: with no pretensions, no false personalities, no facades; just being utterly nude as you are, utterly naked in your reality. The moment you can gather that much courage you will be so filled with joy…you cannot believe right now, you cannot even conceive right now, because it is our falsities which are like parasites on our being; they go on sucking our blood. The more falsities you create around yourself, the more miserable you become, the more you are in a hell. To live in falsities is to live in hell: to live authentically is to be in heaven.

Regret

You regret because you never do things wholeheartedly, you are always divided. Some part of you wants to do it, some part of you is against doing it. If you do it, the part that was against is going to make you regret. If you do not do it, the part that was for it is going to make you regret.

Ego

The ego is just the opposite of your real self. The ego is not you. The ego is the deception created by the society so that you can continue playing with the toy and never ask about the real thing. That's why my insistence that unless you drop the ego, you will never come to know yourself.

Receptivity

You have to understand the importance of being open and receptive to whatever life brings. What is receptivity? Receptivity is a state of no-mind. When you are utterly empty of all thought, when consciousness has no content, when the mirror of consciousness reflects nothing, it is receptivity. Receptivity is the door to the divine.

Receptivity simply means dropping the garbage that you go on carrying in your head. And there is much garbage, utterly useless.

Difference between watching and witnessing

There is a difference. You watch television, you don't witness it. But, while watching television, if you start witnessing yourself watching television, then there are two processes going on: you are watching television, and something within you is witnessing the process of watching television. Witnessing is deeper, far deeper. It is not equivalent to watching. Watching is superficial. So remember that meditation is witnessing.

Truth being simple

Truth is simple and truth is difficult. In fact it is difficult because it is simple. It is so simple and your minds are so complicated that you cannot understand it, you go on missing it. It is so simple that it gives no challenge to you. It is so simple that you pass by the side of it remaining completely unaware that you have passed truth. Truth is simple because truth is obvious. But simple does not mean easy. The simplicity is very complex. If you enter in it you will be lost, you may never be able to get out of it.

That simplicity has depth in it, it is not shallow. And to attain to that simplicity you will have to lose many things — and to lose those things is difficult.

Peaks and valleys

Peaks and valleys will be there. They will disappear only when the conscious effort has disappeared, when the method is no more a method, when the method has become your very consciousness, when you need not remember it, when you can completely forget it and it still grows, continuous, flows, when you need not maintain it, when you need not even think of it – and then it becomes spontaneous, sahaj. This is the end aspect of every step. Remember this: through constant practice a moment comes when you can drop the practice completely, and unless you can drop the practice you have not attained.

4. Most important teachings of my fourth guru Avdhoot Baba Shivananda which I have practiced and applied in my life

• If you hate anyone or anything it means you are attached to it. Forgive and be detached, so that you can be free and happy.

• Baba ji says without attachment how can you hate, the more you will hate the more you will be attached. And if you are detached you are unable to hate also. Hate is attachment driven and forgiveness is detachment driven. If you forgive the person you hate the most, you will be detached and moreover you will save your energy which you were wasting in hating someone. And of course you will feel internally free and happy as you will set yourself free from unnecessary karma.

• When you are free from abuse and praise, in other words when you are no longer affected by praise or criticism then understand that you are rising in spirituality. Baba Ji says that in this physical plane everything exists in duality. The person who praises can also abuse, and who abuses can also praise. They are two sides of the same coin, if one is there; the other is bound to occur sooner or later. When a person understands this and is unaffected by abuse and praise, he rises in spirituality.

• Whatever you want, you just feel, behave and act that way.

• Don't take away other people's freedom or things that you don't deserve. Baba Ji says, emotions are the source of energy, emotions regulate energy and when we use our emotions to get the things that we truly deserve then it comes to us, like magnet pulls the irons.

• Time is not the reality, it is just an idea or a concept.

- When energy goes subtler or vibrates with higher frequencies, it goes beyond the time and can reach anywhere in no-time, that's why distant spiritual healing works very well.

- Love means non-duality. It means oneness.

- Love is without discrimination, it is the essence of existence.

- Many physical, emotional and mental problems are due to not giving and receiving unconditional love.

- Just try to give unconditional love to everyone and feel and see the difference in your relationships. Unconditional love unleashes the divine energy where all the differences and hatred vanishes and one feels comfortable and loving everywhere.

- The more you think, the less you will vibrate, the lower will be your energy frequency, hence only listen to the language of silence.

- When one starts thinking too much, one's connection from universal intelligence is cut. That flow of light that was coming from infinite, gets disconnected and vibrations of thoughts starts taking its place. Less thinking or no-thinking helps to get one connected with infinite energy.

- Everything is bhava (emotions + intentions) ...."BHAVA RE!"

- Baba Ji says "Bhava Re!" more frequently; Bhava is the word for intentions hidden behind the emotions and they create Karma; good intentions will produce good Karma and bad intentions will produce bad Karma.

- "Karma+ Thought + Bhava (emotions) = Karmayog" this is the proper meaning of karmyog. Our karmas are created by our thoughts and bhava/emotions, so thoughts and bhava/emotions need to be pure and positive.

(191)

- Negative thoughts and emotions create darker energy, and darker energy only creates chaos and destruction. Thoughts and emotions are energy itself, and negative thoughts and emotions are bound to create darker energy and this energy only brings all sorts of unwanted things and problems in life.

- Vak siddhi/power depends on pure intentions.

- Vak means speech, Vak siddhi means whatever one says, come true.

- Baba Ji says that our every cell has its own mind and intelligence, and whatever we think and feel gets stored in each and every cell. And the world is just the projection of our memories or psychic impressions. If memories or psychic impressions are good, world will appear good and if memories and psychic impressions are bad, then world will appear bad. These unwanted memories and psychic impressions are the cause of unwanted mental or physical diseases.

- We can create better feelings and thoughts and replace our unwanted memories and psychic impressions with the newer ones to create the world we want.

- Learn to communicate with yourself. Learn to contemplate and introspect.

- The more ignorant you are, the more you will suffer. And an ignorant person can be easily manipulated and used. To be free from ignorance the best and the fastest way is to raise your level of consciousness by consistent meditation or sadhana.

- Feeling of guilt is the worst emotion. We need to free ourselves from it by inner purification and learning our spiritual lessons.

- We are spiritual beings who have come here to have human experience. This body is not the reality, it is just matter and when consciousness (soul) desires to get some experience then this body is formed. And a soul will keep on coming in the physical plane until it fulfills all the desires.

- People come in your life due to debit and credit of karmas. Here the cycle of karma moves and it will keep on rotating until it gets balanced and to make this balance one has to practice unconditional love, gratitude and forgiveness.

- We react according to our stored psychic impressions in our subconscious and unconscious mind.

- If you will have pure bhava (emotions and intentions) then your anahat chakra granthi/heart chakra knot will open automatically.

- Baba Ji says pure intentions are very necessary to grow in spirituality. All the chakras open itself if you have pure intentions.

- Accept the way everyone is and accept the way you are. 'Accept the way everyone is' means not to interfere in other people's soul-agenda (what they have come to experience in this earth plane).

- Satoguni ego is most dangerous. On a spiritual path a sadhak/spiritual seeker also gets divine powers and knowledge which an ordinary person will not have. The Ego may enhance with these powers and knowledge and is dangerous because it stops the spiritual progress and later on these powers and knowledge are also gone.

- Do nishkam seva/selfless service and you will not be entangled in karmic connections.

- Nishkam seva means service without any expectations. It means you do it and forget about it. It prevents making new karmic connection as well as helps in solving old karmic connections.

- If you do dev (divine) karma in morning and sakam (fruitful) karma in daytime, you will sleep in peace at night.

- Dev karma means karma for spiritual progress, let it be meditation, healing others, helping others or doing any sorts of work which makes you blissful. Sakam karma means karma for livelihood, like doing job or business to earn money.

- Bad karma creates negative energy and this energy destroys our vital force or energy or pranic energy, which is essential for both spiritual and materialistic success.

- In Nirgun state (a state with no quality) you can create anything, but in Sagun (a state with qualities) state you can't create anything.

- Nirgun is at the dimension of formless and Sagun is at the dimension of form. When we do sadhna/meditation and merge with God consciousness, we enter into Nirgun state and from that Nirgun state we can create anything. But in Sagun state we vibrate with less frequency and can't manifest.

- Sagun is a state of duality; Nirgun is a state of non-duality.

- Duality contains pain because in duality the opposite is bound to come like friend & enemy, love & hate, beautiful & ugly. When we accept things and people, the way they are, without any judgments, then duality ends.

- Changes only come by sadhna/meditation and by applying or following guru's teachings in your life because this is the only way to reach higher consciousness and from that higher consciousness anything can be created or changed easily.

So until consciousness rises, no real and permanent change will occur.

- Real test happens when you are with people. If you go to the mountains and live alone, you will never know what karma or weaknesses you need to overcome, but when you are with people you are being pulled, pushed and tested in different ways, then you know how much you have improved or how much you still need to improve.

- Practice silence, remain in state of silence, then you will be in tune with spiritual guides. Baba Ji says everyone is born with spiritual guides but when we are not in silence we do not maintain the needed vibrations to get tuned with spiritual guides. And when we are silent, we vibrate at higher frequencies and can get tuned with spiritual guides. In-fact our spiritual guides are always with us vibrating at higher frequency, but due to not having the same frequency we hardly acknowledge them.

- In the morning, when you wake up, then send 'unconditional love' from your anahat chakra/heart chakra to everybody including all the past and future incidents of your life. Unconditional love is the energy and feeling which can make anything positive and in-front of this energy everything turns to be friendly and favorable and above all it gives a rocket speed in spiritual progress.

- Babaji tells everyone to practice prati prasav sadhna to release all negative psychic impressions or sachit karma stored in their subconscious and unconsciousness to purify their inner self.

EPILOGUE

A lot of people in the past had asked me if they could come themselves or send others to me for guidance, and I had mentioned a few conditions to be accepted before they can come or send others to me. These are the following conditions:-

1. You must be ready to do release sadhna/meditation which is a guided meditation for inner cleansing and purification and be ready to do a guided meditation of unconditional love, forgiveness and gratitude. Be ready to do some amount of selfless seva or selfless work in your day to day life or be ready to commit for it with seriousness and dedication. If you have been initiated into any mantra in the past you can continue to do that mantra sadhna/meditation if it is increasing your peace and harmony. You must be ready to follow my teachings and put them into practice.

2. It is important for you to know whether you can relate and connect with me at a mental and spiritual level which you will come to know after reading this book.

3. You must read my whole blog and in particular article number 1, article number 7 and article number 16 from my blog. My blog address is given on page 197.

4. You must be prepared and be ready to take my strictness & harshness, when I blow, thrash & attack your ego. This only happens with people who lack surrender, faith, acceptance and receptivity. If there is surrender and acceptance, any form of strictness and harshness is not required at all and in that case I can very easily make people aware of their ego and blocks within them which they may not be aware of and are unable to see

and eventually help them to overcome or dissolve their ego and blocks within them.

5. You must come to me with the intention to work towards inner cleansing and purification for spiritual growth & to achieve inner freedom, peace, harmony and to raise your level of consciousness. This should be your main reason or purpose to come to me but that does not mean that help and guidance will not be provided to you in other areas of your life.

If you have any doubt or query and if you need more clarity and guidance on any issue, you can contact me at this email address: findyourtrueself@gmail.com

This is my blog address :-

https://spiritualinsightsandclarity.wordpress.com/

CONCLUSION

I hope this book has served the purpose for which it was written and the readers have got the benefit, help and clarity that they were seeking on their spiritual path.

36312145R00112

Printed in Poland
by Amazon Fulfillment
Poland Sp. z o.o., Wrocław